Life Topics

Home Remedies:
Timeless Prescriptions for Today's Family
Gary Smalley & John Trent, Ph.D.

Adapted for Group Study by
Sue Vander Hook

David C. Cook Publishing Co., Elgin, Illinois—Weston, Ontario

Home Remedies
A *Life*Topics Study

*Life*Topics study version © 1992 David C. Cook Publishing Co.

Home Remedies by Gary Smalley and John Trent, Ph.D., upon which this course is based,
© 1991 by Gary Smalley and John Trent, Ph. D., and published by Multnomah Press,
Portland, OR 97266

Published by David C. Cook Publishing Co.
850 North Grove Ave., Elgin, IL 60120
Cable address: DCCOOK
Edited by Dietrich Gruen
Designed by Bob Fuller
Illustrated by Bruce Van Patter
Printed in U.S.A.

ISBN: 0-7814-9137-1

*Life*Topics

Contents

*Welcome to Life*Topics

Congratulations! You and your class are about to start an exciting adventure. And this book will make your journey even better.

You're about to bring the key concepts from a bestselling Christian book to a group study setting. You're going to turn that book into a fun, life-changing experience for all involved.

We've changed Gary Smalley and John Trent's *Home Remedies: Timeless Prescriptions for Today's Families* (published by Multnomah Press) into a 13-session course for parents. With this *Life*Topics study, it is not necessary to purchase a copy of *Home Remedies* for each group member. That's because this course uses concise, reproducible book excerpts and creative group activities to communicate vital themes from the original book. If you or your group would like even more insights, however, we encourage you to purchase the original *Home Remedies* as a supplement.

The 45- to 60-minute sessions are easy to prepare and easy to lead. Instructions to you are in regular type. Things you might say aloud to the group are in bold. Suggested answers to questions are in parentheses.

Each session comes complete with reproducible Resource Sheets. Some of them are excerpts from the original book. Some are creative group exercises. Some you'll want to photocopy and hand out; others you may want to turn into overhead transparencies. Each session plan clearly explains exactly how to use each Resource.

Whether your group is a large Sunday school class, a small group, a home Bible study, a midweek meeting, or another group, you'll find it easy to bring this course to life. Whether your group members are parents of newborns or of young adults, there is something here for them. Get ready for lively interaction, solid Bible teaching, and relevant life applications. That's the *Life*Topics way of learning.

Terri Hibbard, Series Editor

Introduction

When the chips are down and we're battered by life, most of us find ourselves whispering, *Just let me go home, Lord . . . . Just let me go home. . . . They'll love me . . . they'll care for me . . . they'll make everything all right. . . .*

What kind of home do you want your children to look back on years from now? Will the word "home" stir memories of warmth, laughter, and deep-felt love? Is it the kind of place where your spouse would rather be with you than at work or with others . . . the kind of place where hurting friends and neighbors find God's love and support?

In a loving home, there is hope and healing, help and health. Supportive arms hug away our hurts, voices cheer us on, smiles light up our eyes, and tears of compassion soothe us when we've failed. Even in the longest, darkest night, the porch light is always lit, always showing the way to the one place where love is given freely, not earned or demanded.

—Smalley and Trent

(Excerpted by permission from *Home Remedies,* © 1991 by Gary Smalley and John Trent and published by Multnomah Press.)

THE FOUNDATION FOR ALL LOVING RELATIONSHIPS

Session 1

What does it mean to "treasure" another human being? Is it just so much flowery talk—or does it cut into the bone and sinew of life itself?

To treasure something means to attach great importance or high value to it. People take good care of what they treasure. Have you noticed it?

If your hobby is restoring classic cars, you probably don't let your teenager take them off-road to jump gullies in the desert. If you're a stamp collector, you know how to pick up those precious little squares with special tweezers and ever-so-gently slip them into protective sleeves.

People take time with what they treasure. If you're a football fanatic, your Saturdays, Sundays, and Monday nights are sewed up from September through January. If you do decoupage, each piece of art takes twelve painstaking coats of shellac—with a twelve-hour drying period between each coat.

Based on the amount of care and time you invest in each activity, your family can sense what is truly important to you. . . . With their fine-tuned radar system, a child picks up whether he is more valuable to you than your property or projects at work.

—Smalley and Trent

YOU'RE AIMING TO . . .
- Discover what it means to treasure God and family while still valuing yourself.

YOU'LL STUDY . . .
- Deuteronomy 6:5-9; Matthew 22:34-39; Romans 12:10; Philippians 2:3, 4
- Major themes from Chapter 1 of the book *Home Remedies*

YOU'LL NEED . . .
- Bibles
- Copies of Resource 1A, "Shopping Spree"
- Copies of Resource 1B, "A Play on Family Life"
- Copies of Resource 1C, "Scripture Search"
- Pencils
- Whistle or buzzer (as a prop, your own mouth will do)
- Ball and a big book (to use as props)

Step 1 *(10 minutes)*

Setting Priorities
What's Important to You?

When all group members are present and seated, you may begin by asking something like: **What is really important to you? Would you rather spend an entire Saturday on the golf course or an uninterrupted day with your kids? Would you rather have your dream car or take a getaway weekend with the kids?** (You may select other questions, more suitable to your group, from among those listed on Resource 1A.) Then introduce the first activity: **Let's go on a Shopping Spree to discover our priorities.**

Handout "Shopping Spree: What's *Really* Important to Me?" (Resource 1A). Read aloud the instructions and have everyone complete it on his or her own. After 3 minutes, "blow the whistle" (or sound a buzzer) and invite discussion about what's important by asking:

What did you spend the most money on?
Which of your priorities surprised you?
What do you think you *should* have spent the most money on? Why?
How do your priorities affect your children?

After listening to responses, have a volunteer read the quote from Smalley and Trent at the bottom of Resource 1A. Explain that the course you're starting is based on the book *Home Remedies* (Multnomah Press), written by Gary Smalley and John Trent. Through best-selling books, films, and national seminars, the authors have brought hope and healing to thousands of homes. Quoting from the cover jacket:

"(The course and) the book offer timeless prescriptions that have proven effective for a wide variety of family ailments. They offer solid help and encouragement . . . proven principles that really work . . . and practical wisdom that's rooted in the Scriptures. If you apply these principles in your home, they *will* make a difference!"

Step 2 *(15-20 minutes)*

What about Family?
Spending Time Treasuring One Another

Introduce the next activity by asking parents about their real priorities when it comes to spending time with their kids. **Where do our children and spouse fit into our priorities and our daily schedules? Are we letting them know how valuable they are to us? Are we committed to them unconditionally? Are we scheduling special family times together? Does our family know we're available to them at *any* time?**

Let's enter a typical home right now—maybe you'll recognize someone in *your* family in this role play.

Hand out "A Play on Family Life" (Resource 1B). Ask for two group members to assume the roles and read through it. (NOTE: You may want to recruit volunteers in advance.) After the skit, hand out copies of Resource 1B to the entire group. Have a volunteer read the quote from Smalley and Trent.

Does anyone have any examples from firsthand experience to share along these lines?

After a few moments of sharing, read the following list of activities one at a time. Have the group members think of the last time they did or how often they do each activity or one that would be an equivalent.

Told my kids or spouse how valuable they are to me.

Gave up a TV show so I could play with my child(ren).

Read a book to my child.

Talked to my child for ten minutes without distractions.

Played a board game (Scrabble, Chutes and Ladders) with my child(ren) or spouse.

Went out for ice cream or a coke date with a child alone.

Took a walk with my child(ren) instead of my pet.

Gave an extra word of praise for a chore well done.

Asked my child(ren) to tell me their dreams or fears.

Judging from when you last did something, or how often you do it, what is most important or valuable to you? (Be honest!) Where then do you spend most of your unscheduled time? Who or what gets your undivided attention?

 *Step 3* *(20 minutes)*

Where's Your Heart?
Searching Scripture for Right Relationships

Divide the group into three subgroups (subgroups can be just two or three people if your group is small). Assign one of the following Scriptures to each group:

Group A. Matthew 22:34-39

Group B. Deuteronomy 6:5-9

Group C. Romans 12:10; Philippians 2:3, 4

Hand out "Scripture Search" (Resource 1D). Give the groups 5-10 minutes to answer and discuss the questions. Then have the subgroups report to the entire group, summarizing the text and giving their answers to the questions.

Here are some suggested answers to the questions:

Group A: Matthew 22:34-39

1. To love the Lord your God with all your heart, soul and mind.

2. We should love God so much that He is in the center of everything we do, feel and think. If God's perfect love were in everything we did, felt and thought, we would be loving our family with God's love.

3. We can't really love others unless we are loving God.

4. I'd be more patient and tolerant. I'd give them the biggest pieces of cake. I'd forgive their failures quickly and encourage them to try again. I'd empathize with their sorrows and celebrate with their successes.

Group B: Deuteronomy 6:5-9

1. Total, unconditional. He should be the center of everything we do, feel and think.

2. Make God the center of all my activities and relationships; memorize Scripture.

3. We should share God's love and commands with our children.

4. God's love would be in that parent's actions and words. Children would be reacting to God's love, not to our own selfish ambitions.

Group C: Romans 12:10; Philippians 2:3, 4

1. We should love all others (including family, co-workers, neighbors, etc.).

2. The interests of others should also be considered.

3. I'd spend more time with my kids; I'd be nicer when I talk to my spouse; I'd tell my family what they mean to me, etc.

4. I could spend some time talking; go out somewhere with them; give up one of my activities to go on a walk with my teenager; make cookies with one of my kids; play catch with my kids; take my spouse out to dinner.

Close the session with this statement: **Treasuring others (especially family) above ourselves will send a valuable message to our kids that they'll never forget! What is more, loving God first and foremost will change our relationship with our family.**

SHOPPING SPREE: WHAT'S REALLY IMPORTANT TO ME?

You have $100 to spend. The least you can spend on any one item is $10. The most is $100 on just one thing. Read through the list and decide which things are most important to you. Fill in the amount you are willing to spend for each of these items. Work fast—trust your impulses. This is a shopping spree—3 minutes max.

$_____ A 10% increase in the family income

$_____ A true Sabbath rest from all duties so that I can worship God

$_____ Get away weekend with the kids

$_____ Use of my dream car for one week

$_____ Time to help my kids with homework

$_____ Time to make Christmas decorations or cookies as a family

$_____ Time to complete that unfinished house project as a family

$_____ Uninterrupted time to read a good book alone

$_____ Weekly "family night"

$_____ Time to read a good book to my kids

$_____ Time to take a walk with my teenager

$_____ A weekend alone with my spouse

$_____ An hour just to be quiet with God

$_____ A free Saturday to spend on my favorite hobby, all by myself

$_____ A special day golfing (skiing or whatever) with one of my kids

$_____ An evening set aside to listen to my kids' dreams and fears

$_____ One uplifting time of table devotions as a family

$_____ One stress-free day (50% reduced sibling rivalry, time alone)

$_____ Obedient children (just for one day)

$_____ Solid night's sleep, two nights in a row

$_____ **Total (must be $100)**

BONUS QUESTION: Is there any other item that you would add to this list?

Where Your Treasure Is. . .

We would be the first to admit that it's easy to talk a good game here. It's easy to say we "value" our relationship with Christ. It's easy to affirm that our spouses or families are "important" or "precious" to us. We convince ourselves that this is true. But what does the record really show? Where are we *actually* investing the cream of our time and thoughts and energies? THAT is what we really treasure. . . .

You may never have all the goodies, gadgets, and material "treasures" you've wished for and wanted over the years. Your residence may never make the pages of *House Beautiful* and your story may never be told on "Lifestyles of the Rich and Famous." But have no doubt: there is treasure, real treasure, in the homes of those who turn against the current of popular culture and determine to place a high value on God and their family.

A Play on Family Life

"To treasure something means to attach great importance or high value to it. People take good care of what they treasure. Have you noticed it?. . . Without meaning to, a parent or spouse can communicate nonverbally that other people or activities are more important to him or her than family."

—*Smalley and Trent*

Now we enter the home of **DADDY,** with big book, and his **CHILD,** about five years old, and eager to play ball.

CHILD: Daddy, throw the ball to me!

DADDY: *(engrossed in his reading)* Uh huh.

CHILD: Okay, Daddy, let's go. I can throw really far and catch the ball from really far away. Here, Daddy, catch. *(Throws ball at Daddy, hitting his book.)*

DADDY: Hey, no throwing balls in the house! You take that ball outside. This book cost $19.95 plus tax! You've *got* to learn to take good care of books so they'll last forever.

CHILD: Would you throw the ball to me, Daddy?

DADDY: Pretty soon.

CHILD: *(Waits patiently, trying to throw the ball and catch it alone.)* Come on, Daddy, let's play ball! When are you going to be done with your book?

DADDY: It will take a while—there's, let's see, 864 pages. It's really a great book. Someday you'll be reading big books just like daddy! I'll save this one for you. It's the sequel to *Gone With the Wind*—well, I guess you don't know about that book yet either—but you'll grow up soon, son, and you'll realize the value of a good book.

CHILD: Daddy, would you throw the ball to me?

DADDY: *(engrossed in his reading again)* Hmmm?

CHILD: *(pushing away book)* Daddy, which do you love most—that book or me?

SCRIPTURE SEARCH

Group A: Matthew 22:34-39

1. From this text, what does Jesus consider to be the greatest commandment?

2. In your own words, explain just how much we're supposed to love God. How might loving God this much change the way you love your family?

3. Why does loving others take second place to loving God?

4. How would you treat your family differently if you loved them as yourself?

Group B: Deuteronomy 6:5-9

1. From this text, what kind of love does God expect from us?

2. How can God's commands be on your heart?

3. With whom should we be sharing God's love and commands?

4. Suppose parents loved God with all their heart, soul, and strength. How might that change their family life?

Group C: Romans 12:10; Philippians 2:3, 4

1. Who should you honor above yourself and why?

2. Whose interests should you consider other than your own?

3. How would your priorities be different at your house tomorrow if you honored your spouse and children above yourself?

4. What can you do to show more interest in one family member this week?

AFFIRMATION AND TOUCH

Even the smallest act of affirmation can bring large benefits to a child. How tiny those seeds can be! A woman we know had a very poor self image as a junior higher. Because of several childhood illnesses, she was pale, thin and underdeveloped for her age. An alert pastor's wife, however, found something to compliment: "Teri, you look so good with that red hairband. I think red really compliments you!"

The comment only took a few seconds and is now decades in the past. The junior high girl is now a wife and mother. Yet if you would look in her closet, you would immediately see a predominance of red. She has felt good about herself wearing that color ever since.

Opportunities to affirm are varied, but it takes an awake, perceptive parent to maximize the moment. Kids look to their parents to put the events of their lives—the ups and downs—in context. Mom and Dad have the opportunity to *frame* and give meaning to such occurrences. It takes a loving, attentive parent to take a common stone and make it into a *milestone* in a son or daughter's life.

—Smalley and Trent

YOU'RE AIMING TO . . .
- Urge parents to affirm their children through word and touch.

YOU'LL STUDY . . .
- Proverbs 25:11; Matthew 5:1-12 and 8:1-15; Philippians 4:5
- Major themes from Chapters 2 and 3 of the book *Home Remedies*

YOU'LL NEED . . .
- Bibles
- Resource 2A, "My Kid's Great"
- Resource 2B, "A Really Big Deal"
- Resource 2C, "When Touch Is Withheld"
- Pencils
- Chalkboard and chalk or newsprint and markers

Step 1 (5-10 minutes)

My Story
Sharing Your Own Experiences with Affirmation

As this session begins, jot this question on the board, or on newsprint:
When you were a child, did you receive more *praise,* or more *criticism,* from your parents?

Encourage many people to give a short answer to this question. Allow more time for some to tell their own story. Encourage stories of the positive effects of praise, as well as the negative effects of criticism.

Then ask: **Do you GIVE more *praise,* or more *criticism,* to your own children?** (For now, don't give time for answers—only contemplation.)

Step 2 (10-15 minutes)

My Kid's Great
Affriming My Child

Introduce this activity by recognizing how easy it is to find reasons to criticize or correct our children. When they suffer from an unrealized potential or chronic mediocrity, that's when they desperately need our affirmation or encouragement. That's also when we're often at a loss for words. **Let's explore the positive traits in our children. Every child has talents. Positive things can be found in every child's actions and personality.**

Hand out "My Kid's Great" (Resource 2A) and allow 5-10 minutes for each person to complete it. Instruct them to make a list for *each* of their children (those with fewer children can have longer lists). Some suggestions for the list might be:
- throws or catches a ball really well
- creates many new things from scratch
- draws well, listens well, etc.
- performs well in math, music, etc.
- has capabilities for leadership, humor, etc.

Have a few volunteers share some of their answers. Ask a quiet member of the group to read the three pointers from Smalley and Trent at the bottom of the page.

What Can I Do?
Making the Most of Your Child's Accomplishments

Smalley and Trent have said of parents, "You have the awesome opportunity to immortalize moments in your child's life."

What has your child done lately that amazed you? That pleased you? What have you said to your child(ren) lately that has changed their attitude about themselves?

Affirmation can also be silent. Without a word, a parent can encourage, strengthen, and comfort a child—just by meaningful touch.

Divide the group in half. If you want to increase discussion even further, divide each your group into smaller groups of 2 or 3. Give half the groups, "A Really Big Deal" (Resource 2B); and the other half, "When Touch Is Withheld" (Resource 2C). Have the groups read their respective stories to themselves, then discuss the questions at the bottom among themselves.

Bring the groups back together again and have a volunteer summarize each story. Then discuss the answers to the questions as a whole group, giving as many people an opportunity to share as time permits.

Our children look to us for both affirmation and meaningful touch.

The Encouraging Word
Jesus—Our Example of Affirmation

Introduce this next activity by holding up a Bible and saying: **God's Word encourages us to affirm each other and treat each other with a gentleness that sometimes only comes from meaningful touch.**

Have someone read Proverbs 25:11. Ask, **What does this verse say to us about affirmation?** (At the right time, words bring great value to others.) Have another person read Philippians 4:5. **How does this verse relate to the idea of meaningful touch?** (When we are gentle we often hold, hug, or embrace one another.)

We've already read excerpts from *Home Remedies* about how important a "word aptly spoken" can be. We've seen that gentle, meaningful touch is vital to one's healthy existence. But our greatest example can be found in Jesus— the Affirmer.

Divide into two groups. Have one group consider Matthew 5:1-12 and the other Matthew 8:1-15. Each group should read their respective passages of Scripture among themselves and discuss the following questions: **Who does Jesus affirm? What methods of affirmation does He use?**

Here are some possible answers for the *who* and *how* lists:

Group A: WHO'S AFFIRMED?	HOW DOES JESUS AFFIRM?
the poor in spirit	promises the kingdom of heaven

WHO'S AFFIRMED?	HOW DOES JESUS AFFIRM?
those who mourn	gives them comfort
the meek	gives them the earth
those who crave righteousness	promises to fill them
the merciful	gives them mercy
the pure in heart	promises they will see God
the peacemakers	will call them Sons of God
those persecuted for righteousness	promises the kingdom of heaven

Group B:

the leper	touch, words of affirmation
the centurion	praising his faith
the centurion's servant	performing a miracle at a distance
Peter's mother-in-law	touch, receiving her service

Come back together as one group and have someone from each group discuss who Jesus affirmed and how He did it. Others can chime in.

Close by asking: *Who* **will you affirm this week?** *How* **will you do it?**

Ask people to review their responses on Resource 2A and to circle at least three positive things for each child. Encourage parents to tell their children about these attributes this week.

Lead in prayer, thanking God for His affirmation and meaningful touch through Jesus.

MY KID'S GREAT

"The most powerful form of affirmation takes place *close to home*. Words have awesome power to build us up or tear us down emotionally. This is particularly true within the family."

—*Smalley and Trent*

What makes my kid "great"? He or she may have never won any awards or broken any records, but there are many things that make a child great. Make a list of the simple things that each of your children is good at. (For additional children, use back of page.)

Child #1	Child #2	Child #3
1._____	1._____	1._____
2._____	2._____	2._____
3._____	3._____	3._____
4._____	4._____	4._____
5._____	5._____	5._____
6._____	6._____	6._____
7._____	7._____	7._____
8._____	8._____	8._____
9._____	9._____	9._____
10._____	10._____	10._____

Smalley and Trent suggest that you:

1. Make it a goal to praise each child at least once a day for something.

2. "Sandwich" all your criticism between words of affirmation.

3. Be specific with your praise.

A REALLY BIG DEAL

"You have the awesome opportunity to immortalize moments in your child's life."
—Smalley and Trent

A few years ago, I (Gary) watched my youngest son out on that shaky tightrope—and frankly wondered how he was going to do. Through his sophomore year in high school, Michael's principle desire seemed to be remaining *invisible*. His grades were so-so. He was content to stay in the background of things. . . . His motto seemed to be, "Just make it through."

Then, the summer before his junior year, something amazing happened that dramatically changed that attitude right in front of our eyes. At Kanakuk Camp in Branson, Missouri. . . Michael was elected "Chief" of his high school camp, after being one of five nominees in a group numbering over three hundred.

Before the announcement, he was beside himself with excitement at his nomination, yet he always added in every conversation, "Yeah, I know I won't win."

Yet win he did—the first time he had ever won anything in his life. He was stunned! It was unquestionably one of the greatest days of his life. But when I think about it now, how easy it would have been for Norma and me, vacationing in a cabin near the camp, to have minimized or overlooked that moment in our son's life. I might have said . . .

"Huh? Oh yeah, that's great, Mike. Boy, did you see that eagle flying over the lake this morning? Did you see the size of that thing? It must have been . . ."

"Chief? Hey, way-to-go. Norma, did you want to go into Branson and do some shopping this afternoon?"

"Well, let's not get too carried away, Michael. This is just camp, remember? Now if you'd just apply yourself a little harder in school you might . . ."

Michael looked to us to *interpret* that honor by his peers. To put a frame around that day in his life. Was it a big deal, or wasn't it? Did it really say something about his potential, or didn't it? We could have easily—and inadvertently—destroyed that moment by preoccupation with other things. Instead of turning on a light in his life, we could have put that light out, perhaps for the rest of his life.

But after missing too many other opportunities to affirm my kids, I was determined not to miss this one. I almost came unglued, I got so excited about it. We all hugged him, congratulating him endlessly. One of our dear friends, Jim Shaughnessy, pitched in and said, "Great, Mike! Nothing that big has ever happened to me!"

The very next day I went to a local wood artist and had him carve a large plaque with an Indian head on it. I bought some paints and painted the feathers of the headdress, and then inscribed the plaque with a message:

CHIEF SMALLEY
Kanakuk Camp
Summer 1988

To this day that plaque hangs in a prominent place in Michael's bedroom.

But something happened that summer that was more significant than a memento on a wall. The change in my son's life was staggering. You could almost see him say to himself, *Maybe I am capable. Maybe I can accomplish some things.—Gary Smalley*

1. What special "moment" in your childhood gave you an extra dose of confidence? How did it affect you later in life?
2. What "moment" (exciting time) has one of your children experienced recently?
3. What could you do (even now) to make that moment a "big deal"—to immortalize the moment for the rest of your child's life?

WHEN TOUCH IS WITHHELD

"The Power of Touch—we consistently underestimate it. Undersell it. Undervalue it. Underuse it. Yet touch has the power to instantly calm, reassure, transfer courage, and stabilize a situation beginning to spin out of control. To the degree that we choose to employ it in our family relationships, we will push back the threatening shadows of anger, bitterness, loneliness and insecurity."

—Smalley and Trent

The following true story, as told to Gary Smalley and John Trent, bears this out. Read this quietly to yourself. Then answer the questions at the bottom within your group.

The young woman's story seemed all too familiar. She had to do some fast growing up when three major events converged at almost the same time: graduation from high school, a positive outcome on a pregnancy test, and a quick eviction notice from her parents.

The next step was also too familiar. The boyfriend who had impregnated her and spoken with such tenderness suddenly decided he "no longer loved her" and joined the Navy.

Before she could begin to get oriented to the bewildering pace of life change, she found herself with a baby, living in a one-bedroom shack, and working enough hours at a convenience store to pay the rent, hire a babysitter, and put food on the table.

Since there was no one else to be angry with, she became angry with her child—the baby boy with blonde hair so like his father. She was never abusive to him. She never screamed at him and always kept him diapered and fed. She simply decided she wasn't going to touch him.

By the time the boy was four, he had come to associate any touch at all with the fear of anger and discipline. When he misbehaved, he was spanked. That was the only kind of "touch" he knew.

The teacher of the four-year-olds' class knew she had a significant problem within five minutes of this boy's first day in Sunday School. To put it kindly, he was a terror.

This wise teacher looked beyond the little boy's behavior and sat down with his mother the next day. Gently yet firmly, she urged the young mother to talk to their church counselor. After first helping her to see her need of a Savior, this counselor put into her hands one of our earlier books, *The Blessing.*

She read the pages hungrily and very quickly came to two crushing realizations. First, she realized that one major reason she had so hungered for intimacy with her boyfriend was that neither her mother nor father had touched her or shown any physical tenderness while she was growing up. The second thing she realized was that she was doing the very same thing to her son.

Those realizations brought deep conviction. She decided to make a change that very day by giving her son a big hug.

This change of heart made a deep impression on her boy. In fact, it nearly scared him to death.

"Come here," she said to him when he came out of the Sunday School room, "Mommy wants to give you a big hug." The little boy's eyes went very wide and then he took off like a shot. He probably thought, *It's a trick. She's going to catch me and then smack me one.* The more she tried to catch him and hold him, the more hysterical he became.

It took time. A long time. Over and over she would say, "Now honey, I want to give you a hug—just because I love you." Just as frequently he would scream, run away, cry, or try to fight his way out of her arms. And then came the day when he looked at her from across the room, smiled shyly, ran into her arms, and gave *her* a hug. That was the breakthrough in this new relationship between a mom who was learning how to touch with tenderness. . . and a little boy who was learning how to drink it in.

Later she would laugh and tell her counselor, "I need those hugs as much as he does!" They were both on their way to recovery.

1. How many hugs (meaningful touches) do you need every day?
2. When has a meaningful touch from someone helped bring you through a tough situation?
3. How can you do more meaningful touching with your child(ren) this week?

BUILDING CHARACTER

When parents ask us how to teach responsibility to their children, many seem to be looking for a *technique*. Something they can jot down on a three-by-five card. A snappy short-cut formula they can carry out of the office in their hip pocket. SEVENTEEN TIMELESS TECHNIQUES FOR TEACHING TOTAL RESPONSIBILITY. (Now, there's a book title for you.) "Isn't there some kind of cassette tape we can play while they're sleeping—maybe slip it in there subliminally?"

Well, yes. There probably is a book, tape, or seminar somewhere like that. But it's interesting . . . when you open the Scriptures, you read very little about "techniques" in child rearing. What you do read a lot about is *character*: your need of it; your children's need of it; your responsibility to see it develop both in yourself and your family. When it comes to cultivating character and responsibility, short-cuts are in short supply.

—Smalley and Trent

YOU'RE AIMING TO . . .
- Help parents teach honesty and serving to their children in an atmosphere of fairness and consistency in the home.

YOU'LL STUDY . . .
- Genesis 25:21-34; 27:1-36
- Major themes from Chapter 4 of the book *Home Remedies*

YOU'LL NEED . . .
- Bibles
- Resource 3A, "Honesty Scale"
- Resource 3B, "Two Essential Soils"
- Resource 3C, "Jacob and Esau: Case Study in Honesty"
- Chalkboard and chalk or newsprint and marker

The Seedling of Honesty
Planting Truthfulness in Our Children

Begin the lesson by doing a short monologue role play about character and responsibility. The script below involves an interruption by a make-believe ringing of a telephone—a call from someone who wants to speak to your spouse. You assume the role of either a wife covering (and lying) for her husband, or a husband covering (and lying) for his wife.

As parents we're all trying to produce good character and responsibility in our children—and we often do this by merely setting a good example for them . . . (imaginary ringing of the phone).

Excuse me, just let me answer the phone . . .

Oh, hi, Joan. How are you today?

My wife (husband)? You want to talk to my wife (husband)? Well, I'm not sure (s)he's here. Let me check.

(Aside to a pretend, or real, spouse, cupping your hand over the phone as you speak) **Honey, are you here? It's Joan Snyder. You wouldn't talk to her if she was the last person on earth? Okay. I'll take care of her . . .**

(Back on the phone) **Joan, (s)he just left to go shopping (or to the club).** (pause) **(S)he'll be gone for a *long* time. Sorry (s)he is not here. . . . Well, have a nice day.**

What do you think about the phone conversation? Was it justified as an innocent protection of family privacy? Or is this a full-fledged, bold-faced lie? After you get a show of hands—Yes or No—ask: **How can I explain the cover up to my children, who may have overhead this phone conversation?**

(You don't have time for actual feedback or answers to these largely rhetorical questions, as you merely want to set the stage for the following exercise.) **Perhaps, we have "stretched the truth" in some other little ways around the house.** Hand out the "Honesty Scale" (Resource 3A) and read aloud the instructions. Allow five minutes for group members to complete it on their own, five minutes to discuss it as a group.

What seeds are we planting in our children when we exhibit such "innocent dishonesty"? What message are we sending to our children when we encourage *them,* for example, to tell a little lie to escape football practice, or to cover for unfinished homework?

The Seedling of Service
Giving Ourselves to Others

Get your group to decide if they agree or disagree with the following statement from Smalley and Trent (discuss reasons for their opinions):

Serving is another key link in the character chain. If kids can't learn to serve others, they will never learn to be responsible.

What do you think about that statement? Pause for discussion. Encourage a few answers that both agree and disagree with Smalley and Trent's statement.

We often become so accustomed to meeting our children's needs that we don't teach them how important it is to serve others. Let's brainstorm some ways your kids can and do serve others. Wait for someone to share, but if no one is talking, you might suggest the following: Suppose that your child has no money to spend on a sibling's or parent's birthday, but wants to make a gift of time instead of money. He or she offers a gift of a hand-made coupon, which says something like: "Redeemable for two free hours of rent-a-kid service." What two hours of service would such a coupon be redeemed for in your family? Get group members to list other ideas that are appropriate to the ages of their children. List these on the chalkboard or newsprint.

Gifts of time and service, especially when money is in short supply, can be genuine and generous ways of serving.

Step 3 (5-10 minutes)

Fairness and Consistency
Creating Fertile Soils to Grow Responsibility

Hand out "Two Essential Soils" (Resource 3B). Have someone read aloud "Seedling Traits." Why is honesty so important to children? (It builds trust and security.) And what is so important about teaching our children to serve others? (They get the focus off themselves; it helps them be obedient to God's Word; it builds relationships.)

Planting seeds of honesty and service in our homes can only be effective if there is a "soil" of fairness and consistency.

Ask another person to read "The Soil of Fairness." What is unfair in the two examples cited here? (Different standards for parents than children and different standards for different children.)

Does fairness mean the same thing as sameness? (In terms of standards, yes. In terms of relating style, no. In terms of granting privileges at the exact same age for each child, maybe, maybe not. Kids vary in their maturity level.)

What advice would you give to the parents in these examples? (Mom and Dad had better make their bed, etc. The military dad could have learned from his son's resentment and modified his own parenting.)

Have a volunteer read "The Soil of Consistency." Why is consistency so important? (It enables kids to know what is expected; it builds confidence; it makes parents more reasonable and approachable.)

What happens when parents are inconsistent? (Children are put on the defensive. They may feel fearful and insecure. It causes resentment between siblings.)

What examples of inconsistency come to mind from your own home life? What can you do about them?

Family Competition and Conflict

Looking at an Age-Old Problem

Let's look at an example in the Bible of unfairness and inconsistency.

Hand out "Jacob and Esau: Case Study in Honesty" (Resource 3C). Have someone read aloud Genesis 25:21-34.

Review these facts from Genesis 27:1-30: **When Isaac was old and blind he knew it was time to give his blessing to his firstborn, Esau. He told Esau to prepare his favorite dish. Rebekah overheard, prepared the meal, and had Jacob dress in Esau's clothes in order to receive the blessing in his brother's place.**

Have another person read Genesis 27:31-36. Allow a few minutes for each person to answer the questions on Resource 3C. When all are finished, have them discuss their answers to each question.

1. All answers apply. His main problem was (b) that he was a man ruled by his appetites or the desire for immediate gratification.

2. A case can be made for any of the answers, but, basically he was (c) a deceitful liar.

3. (a)—Isaac's favoritism was his character flaw.

Close with this quote from Smalley and Trent: **"Character must be deep-rooted to survive; it reaches way down into the soil of consistent living. It isn't a short term change of behavior that makes an impression on our kids;** *it's a life.***"**

HONESTY SCALE

On the following "Honesty Scale" (from 1-4), indicate how honest you are in circumstances which lend themselves to stretching the truth. Your first task is to be honest—with yourself and before God—as you take this self-scoring quiz. But don't be so soul-searching that these questions stymie you. Your first response is usually most accurate. No one else will see your results.

	For each circumstance below, check the one box to the right (1, 2, 3, 4) which best fits.	SCALE OF VALUES			
#	CIRCUMSTANCES WHICH LEND THEMSELVES TO STRETCHING THE TRUTH	1 = I never do anything like this.	2 = I might sometime do this.	3 = I have sometimes done this.	4 = I usually do things like this.
A	Saying, "I'm not that much over the speed limit," contrary to what the arresting officer has recorded.				
B	Keeping the change, instead of returning it, when the store clerk makes an error in your favor.				
C	Telling all the faults of a used car, used appliance, or some other item you are trying to sell.				
D	Calling in sick (or injured), when you'd just rather not go to work (or a meeting or football practice).				
E	Making up an alibi to escape doing a household chore, instead of telling the truth.				
F	Failing to report all your tax liability, or padding your business expense voucher.				
G	Taking more credit than you deserve for something in your resumé or performance review.				
H	Exaggerating the worth of something you own or have done so that others will like you.				
I	Not telling the whole story if that would shed a bad light on you.				
J	Failing to speak up for someone who gets all the blame for something that you share equally in.				

TWO ESSENTIAL SOILS

SEEDLING TRAITS

We tell parents that if they really want to instill responsibility in a child, they need to concentrate on two specific character traits. If with God's help they can plant these two seedling traits in the lives of their children and nurture them in two fertile soils . . . responsibility will develop as a matter of course. These two crucial traits are *honesty* and *serving*. The two essential soils necessary for these traits to grow are *fairness* and *consistency*.

THE SOIL OF FAIRNESS

You won't be able to teach (honesty and serving) if your children sense a climate of unfairness in your home.

Let's say that mom and dad are trying to establish some basic groundrules in the 'neatness' department. Before the kids leave for school in the morning, the new dictum goes, they need to make their beds and pick up their clothes. That sounds reasonable enough . . . until they happen to pass the folks' room on the way to breakfast and notice that *their* bed looks like Hurricane Hilda just passed through. By the time they've tripped over dad's Reeboks in the hall and removed mom's gloves from the top of the toaster, they could start getting a little cynical.

Obviously, that's an unfair situation. If the parents want their kids to learn some basic disciplines, then they had better ante up with some disciplines of their own.

One of the fastest ways to violate that inborn "fairness" principle is by treating one child differently from his siblings. We heard of one man in his forties who for years couldn't speak a civil word to his younger sister. . . . His dad had returned from the Korean War when the boy was a toddler. Filled with anger and tension over his war experiences, the father was extremely strict with his son, disciplining him harshly. As the war tensions gradually melted away, he became less severe and demanding. The second, a daughter, had a much easier go of it. The father had learned some things about patience and tenderness. The oldest boy, however, was deeply embittered by this change. The dad seemed to be showing preference to the younger sibling. The hurt and bitterness eventually settled into a deep enmity toward his sister.

THE SOIL OF CONSISTENCY

It won't work to give your kids a "weekend seminar" on traits like honesty and serving and then check out for the rest of the year. Character must be deep-rooted to survive; it reaches way down into the soil of consistent living. It isn't a short term change of behavior that makes an impression on our kids; it's a life.

A couple we know have been working hard at planting character seeds in the life of their eleven-year-old foster child. The boy's mother and father are both on death row in the state prison. . . . Our friend is providing this boy's tenth foster home. His life has been a bewildering journey through a kaleidoscope of changing standards. One home strict and severe. The next open and free. One set of foster-parents who are formal and guarded. The next informal and loosey-goosey.

While most kids will never have to endure such a round-robin of parents and homes, many will still face the insecurity and confusion of parental inconsistency. To the degree that they do, their sense of responsibility will be stunted.

JACOB AND ESAU: CASE STUDY IN HONESTY

Favoritism and inconsistency have been a problem in families for centuries. But these two traits can produce an atmosphere of instability and irresponsibility. Read Genesis 25:21-34 and Genesis 27:1-36. Then circle the best answer(s) to each question.

1. **What is Esau like?**
   (a) an outdoorsman
   (b) a man ruled by his stomach
   (c) a sucker for a trade
   (d) a naive brother
   (e) an honest son

2. **What is Jacob like?**
   (a) a homebody
   (b) a mama's boy
   (c) a deceitful liar
   (d) a clever entrepreneur
   (e) a good actor

3. **What was Isaac's greatest flaw?**
   (a) favoring Esau
   (b) marrying Rebekah
   (c) giving the entire blessing to one son
   (d) having bad eyesight
   (e) relying on his nose

4. **Who are you most like? Why?**
   (a) Esau—always coming up on the short end of the stick
   (b) Jacob—determined to get what I want
   (c) Isaac—favoring one child over another
   (d) Rebekah—helping my child succeed, whatever it takes

5. **How can you avoid competition and conflict in your family?**
   (a) treat everyone equally
   (b) be an example of honesty
   (c) be aware of what's going on at home
   (d) outsmart my opponent
   (e) let praise outweigh criticism
   (f) pray my socks off

Be prepared to share some of your observations with the whole group.

MEANINGFUL COMMUNICATION

Session 4

Whenever we teach on the subject of family communication, I (John) sometimes flash back to a scene from my high school years in our single parent home. I remember what my twin brother and I used to do. . . . No matter what time we got in, whether it was 11:30 on a regular weekend, or 2:00 A.M. on prom nights, we would always go into Mom's room, flop down on either side of her on the bed, wake her up, and tell her about the evening.

Sometimes we'd lie there in the dark, talking for hours. It was like stereo for poor Mom, one twin on each side: laughing, remembering, cutting up, dreaming out loud, talking about our plans, hopes, fears, and experiences.

. . . At some point it finally dawned on us that Mom had to get up the next morning and go to work to support the family. Maybe she would prefer that we not wake her up and talk her head off on those late nights. . . .

"John," she said, "I can always go back to sleep. But I won't always be able to talk to my boys."

Did she have *time* to listen to us? Not really. . . . As a rheumatoid arthritic, [she] would certainly have benefited from some extra sleep. The fact is, she *made time* to listen. By so doing, she said "I love you" in a way two teenaged boys have cherished through the years.

—Smalley and Trent

YOU'RE AIMING TO . . .
- Help group members to discover areas where they are weak in meaningful communication with family members and to identify steps they can take to improve.

YOU'LL STUDY . . .
- Proverbs 10:19; 12:25; 15:23, 30; 25:11
- Major themes from Chapter 5 of the book *Home Remedies*

YOU'LL NEED . . .
- Bibles
- Pencils
- Resource 4A, "Are You Saying What I Am Hearing?"
- Resource 4B, "The Listening Parent"
- Resource 4C, "Rating My Words by Biblical Standards"
- Chalkboard and chalk or newsprint and marker

Step 1 (10-15 minutes)

Communication
Developing That Special Art

Open with this Smalley and Trent quote, **"When we stop listening to each other, it's as though our family suffers a stroke. We become disabled. Certain members no longer respond to other members."**

Have someone read Proverbs 15:30 ("A cheerful look brings joy to the heart, and good news brings health to the bones.") **A look can say more than words can express. What are you "saying" in your eyes? Perhaps "I love you!"or "You're in trouble!" or something else? What does your family "hear" in your body language? I'm with you or I'm not here? Do you sound cold and threatening or warm and sunny?**

Have group members pair off with the person next to them but not with their spouse. Explain that one partner should listen intently with eyes that light up, eyebrows that raise at the right time, and body language that communicates interest. The other partner should "listen" without eye contact or any apparent interest in what's being said. He or she should lean back and appear distracted. Let each pair decide who is going to be the good listener and who is going to be uninvolved. Then spend about 5-10 minutes letting everyone tell their partner about their activities this past week.

When time is up, encourage people to share how they felt when someone listened with no apparent interest. Then ask for feedback from those who had a listener with eye contact and expressive body language.

Step 2 (10 minutes)

Listening
Defusing Arguments Before They Explode

On the chalkboard or newsprint, write: Words. Body Language. Tone of Voice. **Which of these three is most important in good, meaningful communication?** Have the group "vote," and tally the responses.

Hand out "Are You Saying What I'm Hearing?" (Resource 4A). Ask a quiet person in the group to read "Real Listening." **Surprised? Let's go on. Some well-meaning family conversations unfortunately spill over into disagreements.** Have three different people read aloud one of the main points. Ask everyone to look over the three steps and circle the number of the one they find most important in communication. Allow for several minutes for people to explain their reasons. **Which one of the three steps is the one you need to work on most? Underline that step. Does anyone want to share about this?** Allow for one or two people to share if they volunteer.

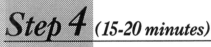

Step 3 *(10-15 minutes)*

Communication Opportunities
Creating Family Opportunities to Talk

Point out that in today's hectic family schedules, oftentimes the only way we can listen to each other is by *making opportunities* to communicate.

One of the ways that Smalley and Trent suggest for opening doors with kids is to set up imaginary scenarios. Here are some ideas to use with your children. Say to them:

Let's pretend you are thirty-five years old.

"Tell me who you're married to!"

"How many kids do you have?"

"Where do you live?"

"What are you doing?"

You'll be amazed at what you'll find out about your kids! Hand out "The Listening Parent" (Resource 4B) and have someone read the opening quote. Have each person individually fill out the checklist. As time permits, have a few people share some of their better ideas.

Do we all agree that today we must work hard to provide opportunities to meaningfully communicate with our families? Move to the next activity without delay.

Step 4 *(15-20 minutes)*

Wise Words
Learning to Communicate Wisely

On the blackboard (or newsprint) write:

Word = a sequence of sounds or letters

Wise = having sound judgment

As we communicate from day to day, we need to prayerfully choose our words or each sequence of sounds so that they reflect sound judgment. That wisdom or sound judgment comes from God's Word, from the God of all wisdom and knowledge.

Hand out "Rating My Words by Biblical Standards" (Resource 4C). Have four people each read one of the four Scripture passages aloud. Pause between Scripture readings to answer the question which follows each one. Try to get different people to volunteer their answers.

1. Proverbs 10:19—How can our words be wise according to this verse? (By keeping them to a minimum—not talking too much.)

2. Proverbs 12:25—What type of words would we be wise to speak? (Kind words.)

3. Proverbs 15:23—What kind of answer brings joy? (An apt, relevant, or timely one—occurring at a suitable time.)

4. Proverbs 25:11—Just how important or precious are words that are aptly spoken

or that are pertinent to the conversation? (Like apples of gold in settings of silver.) Ask someone to put this in his or her own words. (The right words at the right time are highly precious.)

How wise are your words? Look at the bottom half of "Rating My Words" (Resource 4C). Ask group members to go over it individually and rate themselves on a scale of one to ten. Ask them to choose one specific area of communication they need to improve on. Encourage them to start this week.

Close in prayer, asking God to take control of each person's words, beginning with yourself, this week in the specific area each has chosen.

ARE YOU SAYING WHAT I'M HEARING?

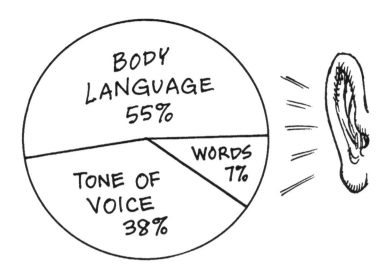

Real Listening

It might surprise you to learn that you listen more with your eyes than you do with your ears. Communication experts tell us that words comprise only 7 percent of communication! Body language is 55 percent and tone of voice 38 percent. So a huge portion of listening is with your eyes.

Real listening means taking some radical steps. Like putting the newspaper down. Or turning off the tube (horrors!) It means leaning forward a little. If the speaker is little, it may mean getting down on your knees. Just imagine yourself five-foot-five living in a world populated by nine-foot giants. It gets tiresome craning your neck all the time!

Real listening means letting your eyes light up. Raising your eyebrows. Expressing your interest verbally once in awhile. . . . Kids will tend to keep talking about a subject if they see someone is actually listening to them. They will also feel honored, valued, and warmed down to their toes.

Quick Listening

Quick listening is one method you can use to help you understand what another family member is really saying. . . . Here are three simple steps to help you get the picture.

1. *Try to "see through" to the issue behind the issue* . . . I can honor you by giving you the opportunity to clarify what you're saying without a response from me. . . . It relaxes you because you realize I'm more interested in comprehending what you say than winning an argument.

2. *Restate what the other person has said in your own words.* After you have had the opportunity to summarize what you've said to me, I can respond, "Now let me repeat what you've said to make sure I understand." . . . It's my responsibility . . . to keep asking questions and rewording . . . until I get a "yes."

3. *Lovingly limit your own words.* Using too many words during an important discussion can actually break down intimate conversation. . . . If I ramble . . . you might become so frustrated or bored that you'll tune me out altogether.

One of the keys to any healthy relationship is a willingness to say, "I'm more interested in understanding what you're saying than in thinking of what I'm going to say once you're done talking."

THE LISTENING PARENT

How often does a modern family "walk along the road" together, enjoying the quiet, pointing out object lessons in the world of nature around them? Those sorts of conversations occurred more naturally in the flow of daily life a few generations ago. Today, we have to work harder to provide such opportunities.
—*Smalley and Trent*

Think of your family calendar for the next month. List two or three opportunities you will **work hard to provide** to foster communication among family members over the next 30 days. To get creative juices flowing, you may piggy-back off the ideas suggested in the first column.

<u>Possible Ideas</u>	<u>Selected Activity</u>	<u>With Whom</u>
• designing your own "one-on-one" or time alone with each person	_____	_____
• going on a family picnic to _____	_____	_____
• taking a long walk to and from _____	_____	_____
• playing a game of _____	_____	_____
• spending an evening at home with no TV	_____	_____
• taking a long drive in the country	_____	_____
• renting a video then discussing key points	_____	_____
• looking at a family album and putting captions with pictures	_____	_____
• pretending you were a book (what kind would you be?)	_____	_____
• dropping by just for a surprise visit	_____	_____
• setting up an imaginary scenario (graduation, marriage)	_____	_____

RATING MY WORDS BY BIBLICAL STANDARDS

Part I. The wisdom of words. Take turns reading aloud the following Scriptures. Answer these questions:

1. Proverbs 10:19—How can our words be wise according to this verse?

2. Proverbs 12:25—What type of words would we be wise to speak?

3. Proverbs 15:23—What kind of answer brings joy?

4. Proverbs 25:11—Just how important or precious are words that are aptly spoken or that are pertinent to the conversation?

Part II. How wise are *your* words?

1. Rate your words (or conversations) with others on a scale of 1 to 10 by *circling* the appropriate number that indicates how you talk *in normal everyday conversations*.

	Unwise								**Wise**	
When I talk about issues with my spouse	1	2	3	4	5	6	7	8	9	10
When I discipline my children	1	2	3	4	5	6	7	8	9	10
When I talk on the phone with friends	1	2	3	4	5	6	7	8	9	10
When I'm at work, with employees, or those I supervise	1	2	3	4	5	6	7	8	9	10
When I'm at work, with my boss	1	2	3	4	5	6	7	8	9	10
When I'm at work, with fellow workers	1	2	3	4	5	6	7	8	9	10

2. Rate your words (or conversations) again on the same scale, this time by *drawing a square* around the appropriate number that indicates how you talk *when under stress*.

3. Which words (or conversations) received the lowest rating? Why?

4. How can you make your words wiser in this area this week?

VALUING AND BLENDING OUR DIFFERENCES

In a recent study of couples married more than twenty-five years, one finding was consistent. Those couples who rated their relationship as close and mutually satisfying had something important in common—they all knew how to value their spouse's differences.

In short, differences can become a devastating source of conflict in a marriage and family. We've seen it time and again. And yet learning the skills of recognizing and valuing each other's differences can be one of the most positive things you do.

Let's face it, learning to recognize and value our differences is a necessity, not a luxury. As our good friends Chuck and Barb Snyder are fond of saying, "Men and women are so different that marriage in itself is grounds for incompatibility!"

When a "very different" husband marries a "very different" wife and they become the parents of "very different" children, it becomes even *more* crucial to understand and appreciate one another's natural strengths. And in spite of our differences, we *can* learn to build family teamwork and harmony.

—Smalley and Trent

YOU'RE AIMING TO . . .
- Show how differences in a family (between spouses or parents and children) can blend to create family unity and strength.

YOU'LL STUDY . . .
- Isaiah 50:7-9; Mark 7:37; Luke 5:29, 30; 7:34; 9:51-56; 13:34—14:6; John 17:4; Hebrews 12:2; Revelation 5:5
- Major themes from Chapters 6 and 7 of the book *Home Remedies*

YOU'LL NEED . . .
- Bibles
- Pencils
- Resource 5A, "Family Zoo"
- Resource 5B, "The Character of Jesus: Four Types"
- Chalkboard and chalk or newsprint and marker

Step 1 (15-20 minutes)

Lions, Otters, Golden Retrievers, and Beavers
Identifying the One You Are

Smalley and Trent write, "Survey after survey shows that the number one reason for mate selection is the *differences* between individuals."

Children each have their own *bent* or unique characteristics. Smalley and Trent stress this point: "Parents who ignore these fundamental differences can unknowingly inflict unbelievable discouragement and pressure on their children." They refer to the familiar Scripture verse, Proverbs 22:6. Have someone read this verse. A good translation of that verse might read, "Train up a child *according to his bent*, and when he is old he will not turn from it."

Let's take a look at four "animals" that might be living in *your* home. There probably aren't any "purebreds" in your "family zoo," but the animals are there!

Have four people each do one reading on "Family Zoo" (Resource 5A). Try to assign the animal parts (lions, otters, golden retrievers, and beavers) in advance to people who somewhat match these four personality types.

Then write the following on the chalkboard or newsprint: **Which animal (or personality type) best describes you?**

Give the group a minute to decide, then have all the lions find each other and form a group, have all the otters find each other and form a group, and the same for the golden retrievers and beavers.

Step 2 (10 minutes)

Mushing in the Same Direction
Roping Our Differences to Work as a Team

Read the last two paragraphs from the introductory quote from Smalley and Trent at the beginning of this session.

When you have all these "animals" in one family, how do you harness them all together so they're all mushing in the same direction? Let's look at three simple prescriptions that the authors have found that work in their "family zoos." Write these three steps on the board (or on newsprint).

1. Realize that your natural strengths are going to expose a different personality's natural weaknesses.

2. Look at the person of Christ as a model of balance.

3. Love accountability.

After two years of Otter-Beaver standoffs in the Trent family, John Trent explains that it was clear he wanted his wife to be an Otter like *him*. And she wanted him to be a Beaver like *her*! They were trying to change each other— even though it was their differences that had drawn them together in the first place. John Trent shares,

"I needed to start valuing my wife for the person she was. Once I made that decision, it was amazing how I began to look differently at her. . . . With the Lord's help, her outstanding qualities have begun to balance out my out-of-balance Otter qualities—and the Lord certainly knew I needed some balancing out."

Why do you think this statement is true? Can you identify with it? Allow a brave volunteer couple to share their story briefly.

Step 3 *(10-15 minutes)*

Model of Balance
Looking at Christ as Our Example

The second prescription for the family zoo is looking to Christ as a model of balance. According to the authors, "During His earthly life, Jesus demonstrated a beautiful balance of each of the personality bents. His love was held in balance. He knew when to be hard on problems, and how to be soft on people." Jesus is a perfect example of a beautiful balance between the Lion, the Otter, the Golden Retriever, and the Beaver.

Hand out "The Character of Jesus: Four Types" (Resource 5B). The large group should still be divided into the four smaller groups according to Lions, Otters, Golden Retrievers, and Beavers. Have each group read their designated Scripture passage and write down how their personality may reflect a portion of Jesus'.

(Answers to Resource 5B can read:

1. Jesus was like a Lion because He was called the Lion of Judah and He set His face to the Cross and determined to go through with it.

2. Jesus was like an Otter because He was eating and partying with tax collectors and "sinners."

3. Jesus was like a Golden Retriever because He stopped to counsel a distraught woman on His way to the cross and He took time to ensure that his mother would be taken care of even while He was dying on the cross.

4. Jesus was like a Beaver because He did things right and didn't turn back from His task until it was thoroughly, eternally accomplished.)

When the groups are finished, ask someone from each animal group to share how Jesus was like their personality. Encourage people to fill in the blanks for the three other personality types. Then ask a few people to describe the kind of person that would have a balance of all four traits. It is important to point out that God is not finished with any of us. As Smalley and Trent say,

"These areas of personality strengths can be developed. The idea that our personality traits are set in concrete may sell books, but it doesn't square with the facts. We've seen in our own lives—and in the lives of hundreds across the country—that people can achieve a high degree of balance in their lives. . . . If we're serious about having Christ as our example, then we need to follow His example of a balanced life and personality."

Accountability
Auditing Family Life

Each of us may try to bring our Lion or Golden Retriever, our Otter or Beaver personalities into a Christ-like balance. That will be hard to do on our own without two things: the power of the Holy Spirit working within us and someone blind-spotting for us. The people in this group can help make the difference if we will care enough to spot-check for one another. Each of us needs to become partners with one other person in this group other than our spouse—women with women, men with men. As partners we will hold each other accountable to allowing God to conform us to the balanced model of Christ.

Allow a few minutes for pairs to get together. Be sensitive to anyone who may be "left over" and quickly join them (or have your spouse pair with them).

Make it a commitment to call your partner this week and ask him or her how s/he is doing with following Christ's example of balance. The authors, Trent and Smalley, affirm the value of having a partner calling in each week for several weeks, in order to break an old habit, to establish a new character trait, or to prune and bear spiritual fruit.

Close the session in prayer, asking God to make each person open to correction, counsel, and insight. Ask each person to seek a balanced Christlike love in his or her family life.

FAMILY ZOO

READER #1: THE LION

I'm the Lion in this "family zoo." I'm a strong, aggressive, take-charge type. My parents tell me that when I got home from my first day of kindergarten I said, "Daddy, I am *not* going back to that school!" When questioned further, I indignantly told Daddy, "because the teacher didn't do one thing I told her to!"

I would rather do than watch or listen, and I love to solve problems. In high school I was voted "Most Likely to Succeed." And succeed I did! As CEO of my company, I've made decisions that have increased sales from $1.7 million to $2.2 million in the first two years. It meant a lot of quick decisions, but they come naturally to me.

In conversation I get right to the point and appreciate it when others do, too. I also expect things to get done right the first time, and the faster, the better.

Some may think I'm insensitive. I've even heard that I need to learn that projects are not as important as people and questions are not challenges to my authority.

READER #2: THE OTTER

They say I'm a playful Otter. Excuse me—the phone is ringing. *(Pretending to talk on the phone.)* Oh, we'd love to come over after the graduation party! What can I bring? *(Pause)* Oh, by that time of night everyone will be ready to eat again. Maybe we should make a full spread of meats and cheeses for sandwiches and have a big variety of desserts. *(Pause)*

Did you invite the Smiths yet? They are a riot when it comes to games. Maybe they'd bring Pictionary! *(Pause)* Oh, sure, I can call them—what's her first name again? *(Pause)* Patti—that's right. Okay. I'll give her a call. This is great. You are the best hostess I know.

(Pretend to hang up phone.)

Oops, I forgot to ask what day we celebrate the graduation. And who is it that is graduating, after all? No matter, I'll find out tomorrow.

Otters are fun-loving, relational party animals. We always have a twinkle in our eyes. We don't bother much with details, or the here and now; we live for the future. The perpetual motivator, enthusiastic cheerleader, consummate networker—that's me. But watch out! I attack under pressure!

I've been accused of thinking the deadlines are guidelines. Can't I get it done tomorrow? Sometimes I try harder to be a people-pleaser than a God-pleaser.

FAMILY ZOO (CONT.)

READER #3: <u>THE GOLDEN RETRIEVER</u>

I'm the loyal, supportive, nurturing encourager—a Golden Retriever. Would you like some Girl Scout cookies? I had already ordered twelve boxes, but when that little Sally got a tear in her eye, I just couldn't say "no." Last night we were at a PTA meeting and I noticed Mike alone across the room. I just knew he was hurting or depressed. So I got him a cup of coffee and asked him what was bothering him. I knew it was bad, and sure enough, he just had learned that his dad has inoperable cancer.

Speaking of cancer, I visited your friend in the hospital yesterday. I was really glad you asked me to go see her. I know I really didn't have time to go, as my son needed a ride to soccer, but I just couldn't say "no." I took my son along with me on the way to his practice.

My Golden Retriever son is able to empathize with his parents' hurts. Just the other day, he said to us, "What's the matter, Daddy? You look sad." And later, "Is everything going okay at work, Mom? Are you still worried about your boss being angry at you?" People are always opening up and dumping their burdens on us Golden Retrievers, because we are always-there-when-ya-need-me friends.

Maybe we need to take the advice and just say no once in a while!

READER #4: <u>THE BEAVER</u>

As the Beaver in the "family zoo," I'm detail-oriented, careful, methodic, and absolutely thorough. People often say, "Leave it to Beaver," because I get things done and they get done right! I just got a new computer last week. I am so anxious to start working on it! I've been going over all the directions and manuals. I'll probably get it out of the box tonight. That's what my family counts on me for. Somebody's gotta know how things work, how to re-set the clock on the VCR, what clothes to wash with what detergents at what settings, etc.

If a Lion's motto is "Let's do it NOW," and an Otter's motto is, "Let's do it TOMORROW," then a Golden Retriever's motto is, "PEOPLE are more important than projects." Beavers have a motto, too: "If we're going to do it at all, LET'S DO IT RIGHT." I want to be able to look back all of my life with a deep inward satisfaction, remembering that I *did it right*.

I guess I can be a little hard to live with sometimes.

THE CHARACTER OF JESUS: FOUR TYPES

Resource 5B

Read the Scriptures that apply to your personality type. Then complete the sentence based on information in the passages. If you finish before the other groups, you may go on to read and apply the other three character studies of Jesus.

1. **LIONS** —Read Revelation 5:5 and Isaiah 50:7-9 with Luke 9:51-56 (Isaiah 50 depicts Christ's path to the Cross).

Jesus was like a "Lion" in that He _____

_____.

2. **OTTERS** —Read Luke 5:29, 30 and 7:34.

Jesus was like an "Otter" in that He _____

_____.

3. **GOLDEN RETRIEVERS** —Read Luke 13:33—14:6.

Jesus was like a "Golden Retriever" in that He _____

_____.

4. **BEAVERS** —Read Hebrews 12:2 with Mark 7:37 and John 17:4.

Jesus was like a "Beaver" in that He _____

_____.

UNTYING ANGER KNOTS

I (John) grew up in a single parent home, deeply wounded and angry over the fact that my dad left when I was only three months old. That left my mother to raise three sons—all under three when he left—and it left a father-shaped hole in my heart.

I can remember hating him during the years when I was going to father/son banquets with a neighbor's dad, and looking up from the football field and seeing all the other players' dads in the stands. But then I became a Christian, and I knew I couldn't hate him any more. So I just "intensely disliked" him. Same emotions, different words, same consequence of darkness. For years I was unwilling to let go of my anger.

While my father was an angry ex-marine, Gary grew up in a home with an angry merchant marine. His father was always angry, constantly belittling and devaluing other members of the family.

Anger from a parent is like a can of red paint spraying out of his or her mouth. It sprays all over the kids, leaving a sticky mess that can take years to clean off.

At different points, both of us had to admit our bitter anger, forgive our fathers, and ask God to wash the darkness out of our hearts—before we spread it to our own families.

—Smalley and Trent

YOU'RE AIMING TO . . .
- Help group members evaluate their own anger in the home and learn to untie those anger knots.

YOU'LL STUDY . . .
- II Samuel 13-18; Proverbs 15:1; Luke 6:37; John 11:44; Ephesians 4:26, 27; James 1:19, 20; I John 2:9-11
- Major themes from Chapter 8 of the book *Home Remedies*

YOU'LL NEED . . .
- Bibles
- Pencils
- Resource 6A, "A Play on Jerry's Anger"
- Resource 6B, "Anger Knots"
- Resource 6C, "Wrath, Revenge & Restraint"
- Chalkboard and chalk or newsprint and marker
- A telephone and two chairs (as props for a play)
- Pieces of 12" string (one for each member of the group)

The Knots of Anger
Learning What They Do to Your Family

State your theme for this session: **What does anger do to a family?** Use this as a rhetorical question or allow a few minutes for group discussion. Group members will agree that bottled-up resentment can be quite destructive, and that anger has many tragic consequences in a marriage or a family.

Let's look in on Jerry, a very strong LION-type. (You may have to refresh some memories by recalling the four types from last week—Lion, Otter, Golden Retriever, Beaver.) **Notice Jerry's anger as he is talking with his counselor and later on when he is at home in a confrontation with his daughter. What does it do to his family?**

Hand out "A Play on Jerry's Anger" (Resource 6A). Select three people for this play (two men and one woman). Their lines are well-scripted, but ad-libbing is permitted, as long as it is consistent with the tone and direction of the original script. Set up two chairs, as if in a counselor's office, for Scene I. Take away the chairs for Scene II.

After the play, ask the following three questions and encourage discussion:

1. Why do you think Jerry is so angry all the time? (He's too wrapped up in his business; he's stressed out; he's never really gotten to know his daughters; he's burned out; he's never dealt with the anger he had as a child.)

After discussion, write this point on the board (or newsprint):

ANGER CREATES DISTANCE

Anger causes husbands and wives, parents and children, to drift away from each other. As Smalley puts it, "Home becomes little more than a dormitory with hostile roommates."

2. In our skit, do you think LeeAnn thought her dad really loved her at the beginning of their confrontation? (Answers could be yes or no. Encourage discussion about why your group members think they do.)

After discussion, write this point on the board (or newsprint):

ANGER PUSHES US INTO DARKNESS

Ask someone to read I John 2:9-11. **Living in the darkness of anger keeps us from being sensitive. It keeps us from loving others, especially our family.**

3. What was the turning point in Jerry's relationship with his daughter, LeeAnn? (Jerry's change of voice tone; Jerry's gentleness; Jerry's asking for forgiveness; LeeAnn's acceptance of her father's apology.)

After discussion, write this point on the board (or newsprint):

ANGER TIES US IN KNOTS

Remind your group: **Forgiveness sets us free** (unties those knots).

Have someone read Luke 6:37. Point out that the word "forgive" in this verse literally means "to release fully, to unbind, or to let go." This is the same word used in John 11:44 when Lazarus came out of the tomb bound in grave clothes, and Jesus "let him go." If time permits, have someone read this verse also.

Smalley and Trent put it this way: Like rope tied around our feet or hands, anger hinders and hampers us. Children who grow up embittered and angry are handcuffed and hobbled, prevented from discovering their potential. Seeking their forgiveness is like releasing them from tight ropes that bite into their lives and cut off life-giving circulation.

Untying the Knots
Realizing the Different Reasons for Your Anger

Pass out a 12-inch piece of string to each person. As you do so, explain as follows: **I'm giving each one of you a piece of string. This string represents you from as far back as you can remember up until now.**

Pass out "Anger Knots" (Resource 6B). **Now I'm passing out a resource sheet which gives ideas for different kinds of "knots" you can tie with your string. Read through the list of anger knots. Each time you come to something that is causing anger in your life, tie a knot in your string. You can be creative and tie different kinds of knots or use just one kind. And be honest! We're all going to have knots in our strings, so don't be afraid to start tying!**

After the strings have been tied in knots, have someone read Ephesians 4:26, 27. **Keep your knotted string with you this week (in your pocket, in your purse, on your car dashboard). As you are thus reminded of each knot of anger in your life this week, ask God to release you. Then as you are released from that anger, untie the knot in your string. Reaching your ultimate goal—a string with no knots—may take months to achieve.**

Seeking Forgiveness
Restoring Relationships with Five Key Attitudes

You may be saying, "I'd love to untie *all* these knots in my string, but I don't know how. I'm fit to be tied."

Smalley and Trent give us five attitudes that will help us untie those knots. These attitudes help us forgive the person we're angry with.

Write each of the words in bold **CAPS** on the board (or newsprint). After each question paraphrase the thoughts below:

1. SOFTEN: How does gentleness or softness affect those around us? Adopt a softened, tender attitude toward the person, never harsh. Go hard or be firm, when confronting *issues,* but always be soft on *people.* Have someone read Proverbs 15:1 and paraphrase.

2. UNDERSTAND: What happens when we identify with or express understanding toward others? As much as possible, empathize or imagine what the other person has endured. Walk in the shoes of the person you're angry with.

3. ACKNOWLEDGE: What is the other person's response when we verbally acknowledge that he or she has been hurt? Recognize that the person has been wounded, even if you didn't do it yourself. Being sure to admit any wrong in provoking that hurt can diffuse anger. Have someone read James 1:19, 20 and paraphrase.

4. SEEK FORGIVENESS: How do you feel when someone seeks your for-

giveness? After you seek forgiveness, you may have to wait for a response or there may be sharp words said in retaliation. Those who are wise will listen beyond the words—to the hurt feelings.

5. TOUCH: Can you think of a time that someone used touch to diffuse strong or negative emotions? Touch in gentle, appropriate ways—on the arm, hand, or shoulder. This is not always easy. At first, the person may pull away. But persistent softness and a forgiving spirit will drain that anger and those negative feelings.

Step 4 *(10-15 minutes)*

Softening the Blow
Learning Not to Sin in Our Anger

Hand out "A Family Remembers: Wrath, Revenge & Restraint" (Resource 6C) and pencils to the group. Introduce this activity by saying: **Scripture gives us a powerful example of an angry family relationship in II Samuel 13-18. The long story has been summarized for us in Resource 6C.** Read the directions and then have someone read this true story with as much passion and drama as possible. As the story is being read, have everyone else circle or mark their answers to the four search questions.

When the group is finished with Resource 6C, discuss the answers. Possible answers include:

1. Who is angry in this story? (Tamar, Absalom, David, Joab.)

2. Who had a *"right"* to be bitter and seek revenge? (Tamar, David.)

3. Who sins in his anger? (Absalom, Joab.)

4. Who does not allow his anger to ruin the rest of his life? (David.) **How does he overcome his anger?** (He forgives Absalom; he doesn't become bitter; he trusts God to lead him; he exercises godly restraint.)

Trent and Smalley suggest: "Since our parenting time is so brief, let's not allow precious days and weeks and months to be shadowed by the bitterness and separation of unresolved anger. With God's help, let's take the initiative to untie the knots . . . while we still can.

Have someone read the last paragraph on Resource 6B. Close with prayer for God's enabling power to untie some knots this week.

A PLAY ON JERRY'S ANGER

<u>Cast of Characters:</u>

Jerry:	Father of three teenaged daughters
Gary:	Jerry's counselor
LeeAnn:	Jerry's middle daughter

Scene I: Gary's Counseling Center, with two chairs facing the audience at an angle.

Gary: So you have three teenaged daughters—all beautiful girls from what I hear—and they're pulling away from you.

Jerry: *(a little afraid)* Yes.

Gary: Because of your harshness; because of your anger. Is that right, Jerry?

Jerry: Yes.

Gary: And you're afraid that boys are going to take advantage of that situation—that you are actually pushing your girls into the arms of their boyfriends?

Jerry: Well . . . yes.

Gary: Jerry, you're exactly right. That's exactly what's going to happen. It's probably happening already.

(Jerry is shaken and puts his head in his hands.)

Gary *(turns and talks just to group without Jerry hearing)*: Jerry was deeply involved in building his own business through most of the girls' growing up years. He worked long hours, weekends, and rarely took vacations. A strong "Lion" temperament type, he liked "laying down the law" and roaring out commands. Tenderness did not seem to be in his vocabulary. As a result, he had filled his daughters' hearts with anger.

Gary: *(back to Jerry again)* I'm not going to kid with you, Jerry. I'm going to flat tell you. You're going to lose your girls. Probably all of them. You don't have a chance unless you start making some massive changes *now*. And even now it may be too late.

Scene II: Two days later at Jerry's home, with LeeAnn standing with phone propped up to her ear, her back turned away from her dad.

Jerry: *(to LeeAnn, injecting himself in front of her)* No! That's enough! Maybe you need ALL your phone privileges revoked. Yeah—maybe you need to stay off that phone completely for a couple weeks. Yeah, I think you do. And that's the way it's gonna be—get used to it!

(LeeAnn runs off crying—to get away from him.)

Jerry: *(to himself, but with eyes looking up)* Dear God, I'm doing it again! It's just like Smalley said. I'm pushing her away from me. I've got to do something right NOW because I don't want any more anger in her heart.

Jerry: *(to his daughter)* LeeAnn, honey. Daddy was so wrong to say what I just said. *(Pause)* LeeAnn. What I just did was so bad. I should not say those kinds of things. I'm so sorry for the way I've treated you. I love you, LeeAnn. Would you . . . could you forgive me?

LeeAnn: *(after a long pause and rather hesitantly)* Yes, Daddy, I will. Oh, Daddy, I do forgive you! *(Embrace)*

ANGER KNOTS

Here are some possible reasons for anger in your life. When you come to something that is causing you to be angry, tie a knot in your string. (You can fill in additional reasons for anger on the blank lines at the bottom.)

- ☐ I loved someone very much—and that person died.
- ☐ I don't like my job.
- ☐ I don't have a job.
- ☐ I was passed over for a promotion at work.
- ☐ My spouse criticizes me too much.
- ☐ My parents are not pleased with me.
- ☐ I have to work too much.
- ☐ My marriage failed (or is failing).
- ☐ My spouse doesn't understand me.
- ☐ My kids don't listen to me.
- ☐ I can't have kids.
- ☐ One of my children is in trouble (drugs, sex, etc.)
- ☐ I can't forgive myself for a big mistake I made.
- ☐ My dad (or mom) left when I was young.
- ☐ My parents always belittled me.
- ☐ I can't forgive _____ for what was done to me.
- ☐ My friends don't care.
- ☐ My kids don't respect me.
- ☐ I'm adopted.
- ☐ I was abused as a child.
- ☐ Other: _____
- ☐ Other: _____
- ☐ Other: _____

"In your anger do not sin: Do not let the sun go down while you are still angry, and do not give the devil a foothold" (Ephesians 4:26, 27, NIV).

Keep your knotted string with you this week (in your pocket, in your purse, etc.). As you deal with each area of anger in your life, ask God to release you. Then as you are released from that anger, untie the knot in your string. Your ultimate goal, even if it takes months: *A string with no knots!*

A FAMILY REMEMBERS: WRATH, REVENGE, & RESTRAINT

Resource 6C

by Sue Vander Hook

This true story, as told to the prophet Samuel, is recorded in II Samuel 13–18. As you read, answer the following questions and draw your circles on this page.
*(1) Who is angry?—draw circles and label each with an **A***
*(2) Who had a right to be bitter and seek revenge?—circle and label with an **R***
*(3) Who sins in their anger?—circle and label with an **S***
*(4) Who doesn't allow anger to ruin his entire life?—circle and label with **N/A***
(Bonus Question: How does he overcome his anger?)

Among King David's children were his daughter, Tamar, and his two sons, Amnon and Absalom. One day Amnon rapes his own half-sister Tamar. Absalom finds out about it and not only harbors his sister Tamar in his house, but harbors his anger against Amnon for two years.

Then Absalom devises a plan to get rid of Amnon. At a banquet for all the brothers, Absalom orders his men to kill the drunken Amnon. And the order is carried out.

King David hears about his son's murder and goes into deep mourning. Meanwhile, Absalom fears his father and flees to Geshur for three years. David finally gets over the shock of Amnon's death and yearns for Absalom.

The plot develops behind the scenes. Joab hires a woman to dress up as though she's in mourning and to go to King David with "her own" contrived story about her two sons who get into a fight—and one kills the other. She asks David to help the son who killed his own brother—to save him from those in her family who want to put him to death. David issues a decree that no one can harm the son. Then the woman "blows her cover" and turns the tables back to David's own situation with Absalom. David realizes then that he needs to accept Absalom back into his family.

Through more scheming, Joab gets Absalom to return to his father. But the father/son conflict doesn't stop here. Absalom persuades the people to follow his leadership, undermining his father's rule, until it becomes a full-fledged conspiracy against King David. So David leaves his throne and his city behind and flees to the country. As David tries to leave the city, one of Absalom's followers throws rocks at David, curses him, and tells him to get out. Yet David does not fight back. He depends on the Lord to see his distress and work things out for good.

Absalom continues his plan against his father and agrees to have him attacked and killed. But David's army proves stronger, and defeats Absalom's army that day. Absalom, still alive after the battle, rides his mule under the thick branches of an oak tree, where his hair gets caught. He's left hanging in midair. David's men leave him hanging there alive, but an angry Joab plunges three javelins into his heart.

When David hears of Absalom's death, he cries as never before.

Resolving Conflict

It was a blended family that wasn't blending. . . .

An alarmed friend of the couple strongly suggested they attend one of our "Love Is a Decision" seminars being held in Phoenix that weekend. As a last resort, they decided to make the two hour drive and attend.

They almost never made it.

Round One of their sharpest argument yet began nine miles out of town on I-10 just past the Maranna exit.

Round Two took them a few more miles down the interstate.

. . . The argument exploded into a savage shouting match.

That sinks it, the husband thought. *I'm not going to any "love" seminar with this woman. I've had it with this relationship. I'm turning around.*

. . . Wouldn't you know it? They happened to be on a 22-mile stretch of freeway where there simply weren't any opportunities to turn back!

By the time he'd driven the twenty-two miles, they were . . . past the point of no return. So with a sense of weary resignation he thought, *Well, we're already this close. May as well go through with the thing.*

In His grace and kindness, God had not allowed them to turn back on their decision to seek help for their floundering family. They attended the seminar, and the concepts and relationship skills they learned that weekend brought their marriage out of the emergency lane. It was one of the most dramatic marriage and family transformations we had ever seen.

—Smalley and Trent

YOU'RE AIMING TO . . .
■ Help group members handle conflict by attacking the issue, not the person.

YOU'LL STUDY . . .
■ Nathan and King David's confrontation over David's acts of adultery and murder in II Samuel 11–12.
■ Major themes from Chapter 9 of the book *Home Remedies*

YOU'LL NEED . . .
■ Bibles
■ Pencils
■ Resource 7A, "That Stupid Car"
■ Resource 7B, "An Allegory of the Mission Possible"
■ Resource 7C, "Decision-Making Chart" (make extra copies)
■ Chalkboard and chalk or newsprint and marker

Step 1 *(10 minutes)*

The Issue

Discussing Positions and Compromises

Read this introductory Thesis, Scenario and Issue aloud.

THESIS: You *can* keep disagreement from becoming destructive. If the pros and cons of the *issue* are discussed, you can focus on the problem and attempt to find ways to solve it.

SCENARIO: Suppose you inherited $9,000 from your great Aunt Audrey. You want to buy a used Bronco (since your car has 95,000 miles on it and you've always wanted a four-wheel drive Bronco). Your spouse wants to save it since there's nothing in the bank to fall back on and your oldest child graduates from high school next year.

AT ISSUE: What is the best way to handle the money from Aunt Audrey? This is the *issue*—the first level of conflict.

Have group members give the pros and cons of buying a new car vs. saving money. List them on the board (or newsprint).

What are some ideas for a third solution or compromise that would make both sides happy?

If disagreements are kept on Level I only, the *issue* level, and the merits of each position are discussed, thinking through possible compromises, tension can be constructive rather than destructive.

Step 2 *(10 minutes)*

The Person

Learning Not to Attack the Person

Give "That Stupid Car" (Resource 7A) to two people to roleplay a conflict situation. It is recommended that the parts in this roleplay be assumed by two people who are *not* currently attacking each other over money issues. Otherwise, they might get carried away. Have them stop where indicated. The rest of the play will continue in Step 3.

What has happened? (They are attacking each other or the other person.)

As you can see, it doesn't pay to go on to Level II of a conflict—where the *person* is attacked. But there's even a more dangerous level of conflict.

Step 3 *(5-10 minutes)*

The Relationship
Avoiding a Cliff-Hanger or Head-On Collision

Referring to the roleplay you just did in Resource 7A, say: **If we are not careful, our conflict over the inheritance** *could* **end up like this at Level III.**

Use the same two people to complete the last lines of the play in Resource 7A. Ask the group, who may be smiling with recognition at this point, what they thought of the ending. (The relationship has started to crumble over an inheritance.)

Point out that the most dangerous and destructive level of conflict, according to Smalley and Trent, is *questioning the relationship*. This is **"one step away from the cliff,"** as they say.

Ask this question rhetorically (not expecting any answers).

At what level—I, II, or III—do *you* **usually handle disagreements with your spouse?** (Time for the answer will come in Step 4.)

Step 4 *(15 minutes)*

Hard Words in a Soft Way
Slipping in the "Back Door"

Smalley and Trent encourage us to voice hard things in a soft way through the use of emotional word pictures:

"An emotional word picture is a communication tool that reaches both the mind and the heart. It causes another person to not just hear our words, but to actually *experience* **them. This productive skill is helping thousands of families to communicate deeply-felt concerns and ideas in a way that 'breaks through' resistant attitudes and responses."**

Point out that tough messages sometimes seem impossible to get across to someone we love, and word pictures can be useful at such times. (When family members are doing something harmful or destructive to themselves or the family, confronting the situation with direct words may be counterproductive.) **Let's meet someone who had to confront a** *very* **difficult situation.**

Have someone read "An Allegory of the Mission Impossible" (Resource 7B). Then ask: **Who or what is this modern allegory really all about?** (Nathan confronting David about adultery and murder. For those who want to do extra reading to learn more about this story in its biblical context, you may read all about it in II Samuel 11–12.)

Why do you think emotional word pictures are so effective?

Ask group members to silently answer these questions, as you read them:

Who, if anyone, do you need to confront in your family?

What's a tough situation in your family that needs to be handled in a soft way? or could have been handled in a soft way?

How can you come in the "back door" of this situation?

What word pictures could you use to communicate?

Family Affair
Using Conflict to Strengthen the Family

Introduce the next activity with some pitch like this: **We've been talking about conflict between spouses. But** *families* **need to learn to resolve issues, too. Before major decisions are made in your family, and before someone forces a compromise that no one is happy with, think about gathering the facts.**

Hand out the "Decision-Making Chart" (Resource 7C) and ask each group member to think of an issue currently facing them (what car to buy, what home to buy, should we try a different church, should we move, etc.) and then fill out the chart. This activity can be done either in the group or at home, as time permits.

You might suggest that husbands and wives confer long enough to pick a common issue, then complete the chart on their own. That way they will have a head start on a family council about this issue.

Take it home and let the other family members fill out their part before the final decision is made.

Let Smalley and Trent have the last word: **"If you're serious about defeating the arguments and problems that can crop up around any home, try seasoning each day with a liberal sprinkling of praise." Turn to the person next to you and share a word of praise right now.**

Close in prayer, asking God to help each family resolve conflicts quickly.

THAT STUPID CAR

This couple has just received the news that the husband has inherited $9000 from his Aunt Audrey. They are trying to decide how to spend their windfall.

Husband: If you really cared about me, you'd let me buy that Bronco.

Wife: If you had any practical bones in your body, you'd know we should save the money.

Husband: You're being selfish—after all, it's *my* great aunt!

Wife: Why did you get us in such a financial mess in the first place? Most families have some savings.

Husband: You *always* want to make all the money decisions.

Wife: Well, if you could handle money, I'd let you make the decisions!

Husband: You think God gave you the gift of money management? Well, who *makes* most of the money in this family, anyway? What happened to your gift of *making* money?

Wife: We wouldn't need so much money if you didn't spend it on so much junk for your stupid car that has 95,000 miles on it!

[Stop here. Continue in Step 3.]

Husband: At least my car doesn't yell at me! Maybe my life would be better living with my car than it is living with you!

Wife: If that's the way you really feel about it, then why don't you take your car and sleep with it tonight—see how you like that!

AN ALLEGORY OF THE MISSION IMPOSSIBLE

Resource 7B

by Sue Vander Hook

I couldn't believe it! Not my good friend. What a stupid thing to do! I can't imagine he wanted that woman so bad! But let me back up and fill you in on the details.

First of all, I couldn't believe he was playing "Peeping Tom" when she was taking a bath. I didn't think he would do such a thing. And she was even married! He could have had almost any woman in town, and he has to pick a married one. And to top it all off, my friend is her husband's boss! To make a long story short, my friend ends up going to bed with her.

But that's only the tip of the iceberg. This good friend of mine proceeds to set up the woman's husband. My friend puts him on a real dangerous job assignment and makes sure he doesn't come out alive. If it could be proved, I'm sure he'd be convicted of first-degree murder, with motive and everything. But with his lofty tenured position and political ties, it's very unlikely. He'll probably never even be questioned.

This friend of mine lets the woman mourn over her husband for a "respectable" time and then marries her and they have a son.

Since I'm such a good friend of his, I decide to go and confront him about what he's done. But what should I say? The wrong words could be the end of our friendship. But he must be confronted. What he has done is wrong. So I decided to go in the "back door."

I asked my friend to go out to dinner with me. At a relaxed moment, I told him a story about a CEO in one of his subsidiary manufacturing companies who raised large herds of sheep on the side. When the owner of the company came to town, he requested a lamb roasted on an open pit. But instead of using one of his many lambs, the CEO told one of the assembly line workers to bring his daughter's pet lamb for the roast. To save his job, the assembly line worker did what the CEO asked—his daughter's lamb was killed and eaten the next day!

Well, to say the least, my friend was irate! He said he was going to demand that the CEO resign. Then he'd start a criminal investigation into what he did, plus help the assembly worker file a civil suit against his boss.

At that point in my story, I couldn't go any further. I told my friend that *he* was the CEO. *He* was the man who had everything, who could have had his pick of single women, who had position and wealth. It was *he* who slaughtered a woman's only husband and then took her to be his own wife.

I told him that his troubles had just begun. Without arguing or saying another word, my friend admitted how wrong he had been and came right out and cried. What a sad turn of events this whole thing took—and it all started with an innocent bath!

DECISION-MAKING CHART

For each important family decision that arises, let the entire family (even the young ones) fill out this chart. This process will give each family member ownership in the final decision. This will also give each person a chance to voice fears, desires, and hopes about a family decision.

Whenever possible, don't go forward with a major family decision until you've gained a family consensus. Make extra copies of this chart for additional issues and the rest of your family members.

Issue under Consideration:					
Pros	Cons	Lasting Effects of Decision	Is My Reason Selfish?	Will This Decision Help Others?	What Would God Want Us to Do?
1.					
2.					
3.					
4.					
5.					
6.					
7.					

THE GLUE THAT BONDS A FAMILY

It isn't just talking that draws people together. Experts on friendship tell us that people don't become close friends by talking; they become close by doing things together. . . .

It wouldn't take long these days to write a book on "Fifty Thousand Ways to Fragment a Family." Just get out your tape recorder and interview a few of your neighbors, golf partners, co-workers, and relatives. Lots of people could fill the pages in that sort of book.

There's no end to bitterness. There's no shortage of tears, loneliness, and alienation. It's no great task to blow a family into pieces . . . or allow each member to drift away into distant, unrecoverable orbits. But bonding a family together, now . . . creating indelible memories of shared troubles, laughter, and mutual encouragement . . . well, that's the kind of book we would rather read in our old age when all the kids have left home.

What kind of "memory book" are you writing together as a family? Could your little tribe spend an evening of sharing and laughter saying, "Remember when . . ."? Does your book contain any stories that get better with the telling? Do the pages have vivid color pictures of crazy dilemmas, rainy nights in a tent, tipped canoes, water slides, rope burns long healed, and unforgettable shared experiences?

—Smalley and Trent

YOU'RE AIMING TO . . .
- Encourage group members to share experiences with their families, making the most of every opportunity to bond as a family.

YOU'LL STUDY . . .
- John 17
- Major themes from Chapter 10 of the book *Home Remedies*

YOU'LL NEED . . .
- Bibles
- Pencils
- Resource 8A, "The Glue That Bonds"
- Resource 8B, "The Prayer That Bonds"
- Chalkboard and chalk or newsprint and marker
- "Memory Book" with pictures or keepsakes (to use as a prop)

Step 1 *(10-15 minutes)*

Shared Experiences
Becoming Close by Doing Things Together

To set the stage for the discussion you want to spark during this activity, have these questions written on the blackboard (or on newsprint) *before* the session begins:

What makes a close family close?

Is quality time with your kids enough?

How are you becoming better friends with family members every day?

Ask your group to reflect upon these questions *silently*. Hand out "The Glue That Bonds" (Resource 8A). Have a volunteer read "Shared Experiences."

I'd like you to think back, as far back as you need to, to some family crisis —a crisis that you not only survived but that had, or will have, the net effect of bonding your family closer together. What crisis comes to mind for you? (Solicit examples of minor travel disasters, major illnesses or injuries, financial predicaments, a vacation fiasco, a broken relationship, etc.) Encourage short stories—one minute each. **Wrap up your story by telling how (and if) that experience brought your family closer together.**

We usually don't think a crisis can be good, and we usually don't look forward to troubles. But after a couple of weeks, the "glue" of a shared predicament sets—and it bonds us together so tightly that almost nothing can break it apart.

As Gary Smalley says, "It's the family that does things together—enduring the inevitable breakdowns, foul-ups, contusions, concussions, and minor disasters—that ends up being known as a "close family."

Step 2 *(15-20 minutes)*

High Priority
Giving Family Activities a Top Spot on Your Calendar

Ask someone to read "Family-Activities—A High Priority" on Resource 8A. Explain that group members are going to plan some monthly family activity that will help "glue" their family together. They should start with either the current month (if there are enough days left in it), or the next month, and continue through all twelve months.

Thinking twelve months in advance may seem difficult and impractical, but when you're competing with all the other activities in the world, family activities need to get on the calendar first.

When the calendars are complete, encourage the group members to take the calendar home and put it in a conspicuous place (the hallowed refrigerator door, the bulletin board, etc.). Of course, each set of parents can redo another calendar with input from the kids, or with the start-up ideas written in by Mom and/or Dad.

Step 3 *(5-10 minutes)*

One-on-One
Looking for Opportunities to Bond

To set the stage for personal reflection and Bible study, introduce the idea of "memory books." If you have one as a prop, hold it as you talk. Encourage parents to save programs, school papers, favorite artistic creations, etc. for each child. Use a rainy day to put them, along with photos, in a memory book for each child. Point out that whether or not we take actual, on-the-spot pictures, we all keep memory books in our minds.

Pose this rhetorical question, as a lead-in to this study: **Memories of important family events—good and bad—we'll never forget. But what memories are we going to miss out on because we didn't take the time to bond with our children—one-on-one?**

Have another person read "One-on-One Opportunities" from Resource 8A. **Why do you think Gary and his daughter grew so close? Do you think this would have happened if they had not taken that trip? Have you had any similar experiences with your family?**

Smalley goes on to say, **"Whatever the activity, whether going into the hills to cut firewood, driving to the office on Saturday to pick up a computer printout, or walking to the corner convenience store for a newspaper, take one of your kids along. Make the most of every opportunity, realizing that those opportunities are finite and may never be repeated."**

Step 4 *(10-15 minutes)*

The Prayer That Bonds
Understanding Christ's Last Prayer

We see an example of one-on-one bonding in Jesus' last prayer for His disciples—and for all believers thereafter. Have someone read John 17:11, 20-26 about Jesus' desire for the disciples' oneness. Hand out "The Prayer that Bonds" (Resource 8B). Ask people to write out answers to the questions, plus jot down any questions they may have. After a few minutes, encourage your group to discuss their answers.

1. What is Jesus' relationship with the Father like? (They are one—in fellowship, harmony, loyalty, teaching, and intercession. Jesus is in the Father, the Father is in Jesus.)

2. What relationship does Jesus want the disciples to have with each other? (He wants them to be one, although physical proximity or geographic unity is not in view here. He wants them to be unified in purpose and working together.)

3. What is Jesus' desire for all believers? (To be one—in mind, heart, and soul. This doesn't mean unhealthy dependence on each other. Rather, it means that all believers are dependent on God.)

4. Is it Jesus' desire that we be one with each member of our family? If yes, how can we do so? (Yes. By thinking of others first, trying to see things from their point of view, getting to know them.)

5. What family member do you know the least in your home? This is between each person and his or her family.

What can *you* do alone with that least-known family member *this week* to begin a one-on-one bonding process? You may leave this question open for thought, or you may cite your own example; or if the group is close knit, they may feel free to share with everyone.

Close the session by praying for a one-on-one bonding for each group member with the family member they have chosen.

THE GLUE THAT BONDS

Shared Experiences

Ron, Karen, and their two children had been camping in the Oregon mountains. Leaving their campsite that morning, they decided to trek into an isolated mountain lake for a picnic lunch. Nine-year-old Ross and six-year-old Jenny kept up a pretty good pace, but they still consumed over ninety minutes . . . to reach their destination.

Standing beside the quiet lake after lunch, the children were balancing on some rocks when . . . Jenny's sneakers slipped out from under her and—unable to catch herself with her hands on the sharp lava rock—she tumbled full-force onto her forehead.

Head wounds being what they are, there was a lot of blood and crying. . . . With his bandaged girl clinging limply to his back, Ron led the return journey to the car in just forty-five minutes, gently murmuring all the words of encouragement he could think of.

An hour after they reached the car, Jenny was resting comfortable in an emergency room with ten stitches. . . . Ron didn't realize how the incident had bonded him with his daughter until several months later. The rambunctious little girl had yet another fall—badly bruising her thigh. As he was piggy-backing her to the car she leaned over and whispered in his ear, *"Doesn't this seem familiar?"*

Family Activities—A High Priority

There will be plenty of 'good' and 'pressing' reasons to put off a family vacation or camping trip. When the kids get older, family activities run into stiff competition from team sports, club activities, and church youth group trips. Nevertheless, you must decide together as a family that shared experiences are a priority and you will not allow them to get squeezed out of the schedule.

January	February	March	April	May	June
July	August	September	October	November	December

One-on-One Opportunities

I (Gary) remember so well the week I took Kari, then just nine years old, on a ministry trip with me. Something happened during those seven days that I can't explain. Some inexplicable wall that had grown between us melted away—and has never returned.

She was there in my seminars. . . . We stayed together with a family in an old white farmhouse. . . . As we drove the many miles between seminars, we talked about a hundred different things. At other times we didn't talk at all; it was enough just being together. Some of the most precious pictures in my whole memory book grew out of that week.

THE PRAYER THAT BONDS

Read John 17:11, 20-26 and answer the following questions based on that great priestly prayer of Jesus. Choose the responses you think are most appropriate. Or add your own response.

1. **What is Jesus' relationship with the Father like?**
    (a) fellowship among equals
    (b) living in perfect harmony
    (c) a loyal son who has carried out dad's every wish
    (d) perfect unity or oneness
    (e) other: _____

2. **What relationship does Jesus want the disciples to have with each other?**
    (a) fellowship among equals; share and share alike
    (b) priests to one another, no one lording it over the other
    (c) living and loving in spiritual communion as one
    (d) living in groups in physical proximity
    (e) other: _____

3. **What is Jesus' desire for all believers?**
    (a) to be unanimous, of one mind, in our decision-making
    (b) to be uniform, of one style, in our appearance
    (c) to be conformed, of one standard, in our behavior
    (d) to be harmonious, of one heart, in our love relationships
    (e) to be accurate, of sound doctrine, in knowing God

4. **Is it Jesus' desire that we be one with each member of our family? If yes, how can we do so?**

5. **Which of your family members do you know the least? How will you practice the kind of oneness Jesus wants for you in that relationship?**

How to Help Your Family Improve

Only the wise seek and love correction. Only the wise love those who correct them. Is it normal for a person to want correction? Does it feel natural to like correction? No. But only the wise know that it's wise. They choose to be wise by seeking it out.

The wisest companies in the world have evaluation forms that invite correction from their customers. You see it in all the finest restaurants, hotels, and airlines. . . .

These companies ask for constant evaluation. Why? Because they know that feedback and correction from their customers will make them better companies. Foolish companies refuse to change or heed customer input until it's almost too late. (How long did it take Detroit to get the message that Americans simply wanted a reliable small car?)

What then, makes for a wiser family? Do you mail out evaluation forms to your relatives and neighbors? Maybe print an 800 number on the back of your mini-van? *What do you think of our parenting skills? Call 1-800-GET-NOSY.*

Probably not. But for countless families we've observed across America, wisdom is spelled A-C-C-O-U-N-T-A-B-I-L-I-T-Y.

—Smalley and Trent

YOU'RE AIMING TO . . .
- Help group members have the courage to seek help and counsel from Scripture and from other Christians to become skillful at family life.

YOU'LL STUDY . . .
- Proverbs 10:17; 12:1; 13:18; 15:5, 10, 12, 32; II Corinthians 1:3, 4; 2:5-7; Hebrews 4:12, 13; 12:12, 13
- Major themes from Chapter 11 of the book *Home Remedies*

YOU'LL NEED . . .
- Bibles
- Pencils
- Resource 9A, "The Unmentionable Family Secret"
- Resource 9B, "Skills for Successful Living"
- Chalkboard and chalk or newsprint and marker

How Do You Spell Wisdom?
Learning A-C-C-O-U-N-T-A-B-I-L-I-T-Y

What makes a wise family? (You may get many different answers. Accept all answers and leave it open for discussion. The answers that will be covered in this session are accountability, constant evaluation, and seeking and loving correction.)

Hand out "The Unmentionable Family Secret" (Resource 9A). Have two or three people read it out loud.

What might have happened to this family if this one woman had not sought help? (The cycle would have continued. There would have been more pain and silent suffering.)

What if someone had sought help earlier? (Depending on when help was sought, up to three generations could have been spared years of grief and shame.)

Did the daughter betray her family by revealing their "secret" to an outsider? (Encourage pro and con discussion.)

Read the introductory excerpt on page 85. **According to our authors, how do you spell wisdom?** (Accountability.)

The Scriptures have much to say about accountability or seeking wisdom and counsel. Let's see what Solomon says about these topics. Have seven group members find and read the following verses out loud— Proverbs 10:17; 12:1; 13:18; 15:5; 15:10; 15:12; 15:32.

What words are used that suggest accountability? (Discipline, correction, healing.)

What is the person called who does not seek correction? (Stupid, fool, mocker, one who despises himself.)

Who is it that seeks wisdom? (Only the wise.)

The Power Source
Getting Connected

When you're lost, what do you do? Do you keep wandering around—or do you stop and ask for directions? Why or why not? Encourage as many people as possible to answer this question.

Smalley and Trent write, "The best map in the world does you no good if you don't know where you are. . . . *Only the wise stop and ask for directions.*"

Point out that no matter who we are, we all "get lost" sometimes and need to admit our struggles and weaknesses and ask for input and prayer. This will help us improve and grow in our Christian lives.

But where do we go to find someone we can trust when we're lost spiritually or emotionally?

Other than family, who knows you and loves you enough to give you outside support in a crisis?

Who would correct you when you're not on the right track? Wait for feedback. Be prepared to share your own source of support and accountability. Accept all answers and then have someone read II Corinthians 1:3, 4.

Who is the source of all compassion and comfort and recovery? (God is our power, our ever-present comforter.)

And why does God comfort us? (So that we can show others where to find the food, comfort, and support we all need.)

This truth may be illustrated in this diagram. On the chalkboard or newsprint, draw a copy of this diagram:

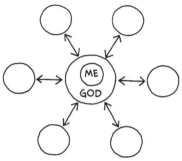

Step 3 *(10-15 minutes)*

Wrap It Up in a Small Group
Networking for Support and Accountability

God has also given us other people in our support network. I am going to read a list of questions. Use the back of Resource A to jot down the name or names of people who come to mind for each one. You will want to make two columns: one for those to whom you turn for support and one for those who turn to you for support. Use the questions below or come up with your own:

Who can you count on to pray for you?

Who can count on you to pray for them?

Who do you turn to in a crisis?

Who turns to you in a crisis?

Who do you trust to correct your kids?

Who trusts you to correct their kids?

Who cares enough to ask, "How are you really doing?"

Who do you ask, "How are you really doing?"

Who can you count on to correct you or speak the truth in love?

Who knows that you will correct him/her if needed?

Who, besides your spouse, really knows the real you?

Who would say you know the real me?

How are you doing? Are the names the same or different between columns? Do you feel you have the support you need?

Some of the group may have an informal support system of friends. Others may be a part of a small group that meets regularly.

Be sensitive to those who do not have a readily identifiable support network. You may need to go over some of the specific questions with them in private, one-to-one.

What does it take to develop a support system? (Being willing to let someone get close enough to really know you; trust; time together; shared experiences.)

Write ACCOUNTABILITY on the board or newsprint. **How do you feel when you see this word?** (Scared; secure; loved; threatened.)

Is accountability something that you welcome? or run from? Why? What does this word mean? (Being liable, answerable, responsible.)

Why is it important to be accountable to another Christian or group of Christians? (Encourages us to be obedient to God's Word. Helps us see where we need correction. Draws us together with other Christians.)

Smalley and Trent talk of two types of accountability—personal and small groups:

"It begins with the first big step of letting someone close enough to you to know what you're really like. Everyone looks good on a Sunday morning at church. But we also need those group settings where we can openly and honestly share the temptations and struggles we face.

"It doesn't have to be a big production. Simply ask one another questions like, 'What are you doing as a family to build love and support in your home?' . . . A weekly gathering with a group of people who love you, support you, and hold you to your goals will give you the courage and energy to make it through the week.

". . . We've not only been in small accountability groups ourselves, but we've given several men across the country a 'blank check' when it comes to correcting us. . . .

"Each of these men knows he has our complete permission to get involved in our lives in this way."

Use this as an opportunity to lead the group into a discussion about small support groups. Discuss how important it is to have eight to ten Christians they can meet with on a regular basis. At this point, encourage group members to become involved in small groups that are available through their church. If none is available, encourage group members to start a support group for themselves and others, beginning with the names they wrote on the back of Resource A.

Have someone read Jeremiah 17:9: "The heart is deceitful above all things and beyond cure. Who can understand it?"

What does this verse tell us about ourselves? (We can fool ourselves; we can thing we're okay when we're not; we deceive ourselves.)

How does this verse relate to the issue of accountability? (It may take someone else to see what is in my heart. I may need help seeing myself. An objective outsider can often see what I cannot see.)

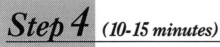
Step 4 (10-15 minutes)

Family Growth
Learning the Skills of Successful Living

Hand out "Skills for Successful Living" (Resource 9B). Have a volunteer read the excerpt at the top of the page. Explain how this parable of the cabinetmaker and the

Scripture references that follow all portray the need for developing skills for successful living. Have the group answer the question individually.

When everyone is done writing, discuss the questions:

1. How then can we become skilled at making a life, not just making a living? (Seeking counsel from those who are skilled. Allowing others who really know me to correct me. Placing myself in a position of accountability.)

2. What happens if you don't get correction? (You continue to repeat the same mistakes.)

3. What is the source of our correction and teaching? (The Word of God.)

4. Why is God's Word so powerful in making us skillful at living? (It reveals our heart, attitudes, and thoughts; it serves as a mirror, revealing who or what we really are; it is alive and active.)

God's Word equips us for skillful, successful living. It encourages, heals, helps us—and our families—grow. Other people, by their calling attention to the Word, keep us accountable and on track!

Close with this prayer: **Lord, please correct me and teach me. Bring people into my life who will correct me in love. Please help my family improve because of the changes you make in me.**

THE UNMENTIONABLE FAMILY SECRET

Nobody talked about Grandfather.

It was an unspoken, ironclad rule.

The circumstances of his passing were a family matter, and family matters were private. Period. You didn't bring up someone else's problems, and you certainly didn't discuss your own.

Grandfather had become ill with tuberculosis; that much the family knew. This was back in the early 1950s and there were fewer treatment options for TB. Some folks went into a "home" to convalesce. Others chose to stay in their own residence and ride out the disease.

Grandfather chose what he considered the "manly" option. He set his affairs in order, drove his pickup into a lonely canyon in the desert, took out his twelve-gauge, and shot himself.

Then . . . it was as if he had never existed. His name never came up again. No one spoke of the incident for nearly fourteen years.

Years after that suicide, Grandfather's oldest son strongly suspected he was developing cancer of the colon. An initial diagnosis pointed in that direction. Like his father before him, he stoically determined that he "should not be a burden," went off to a secluded place, and took his own life.

Another family secret. No one talked about it. Even when the autopsy revealed that this man in his early forties didn't have cancer at all. The diagnosis had been premature—and incorrect.

Scarcely months later, another brother thought he had contracted a debilitating disease. Would he keep this unspoken, deadly family custom? He planned on it . . . but then something happened that stopped his hand just in time.

When news of this man's illness came to light, pressure in the family built like steam trapped in a boiler.

What in the world was going on? Who was going to be next? Lives were at stake. *Yet no one was willing to speak. No one was willing to break a multi-generational code of silence—even when it was killing them.* No one, that is, until the daughter of this man secretly came to me (John) for counseling.

She was the only member of the clan with the courage to admit that something was seriously wrong—deadly wrong—in her family. They needed help. They needed correction. And she was the only one wise enough to acknowledge it.

When this terrible "family secret" finally came to light in a confrontation with her family, it threw them into a tailspin. Being honest for the first time in years, however, was the very thing that finally brought them out of the darkness and into the freedom of God's light.

One woman in a disturbed family had the courage to seek help, and it ended up keeping her own father from fulfilling a terrible legacy.

Skills for Successful Living

"One of the principal words for 'wisdom' in Scripture refers to skill in technical work or craftsmanship or battle tactics. When the Bible speaks of wisdom, it's talking about the skill of successful living. It means *being skillful at life*. If you go to a wise counselor for help and direction, what you're really asking for are skills. Perhaps, like a proficient craftsman, he or she has honed those skills over the years.

"There is a sense in which you can build skill. Yet there are certain skills you may never develop on your own. Imagine, for instance, that you are a 'self-taught' cabinet maker.

"Over the next twelve months, let's say you construct a thousand cabinets. Yet if you build them all with the same structural flaws, you haven't gained any skill as a cabinet maker—despite all your diligent labors. So it isn't just a matter of 'working hard at it.' It is rather a matter of discovering the skills to make it right!

"You may 'hang on' through twenty years of poor family life, but what have you gained? A miserable twenty years. True wisdom seeks out correction and the kind of skills you need to bring encouragement and healing and growth to your family."

FOR PERSONAL REFLECTION:

1. Consider **the cabinetmaker story** as a parable on life. How then can we become skilled at *making a life,* not just making a living?

2. Likewise, consider **Hebrews 12:12, 13.** What happens if you don't get correction and get back on the right road?

3. Consider **Hebrews 4:12, 13.** What is the source of our correction and teaching?

PREPARING FOR TRANSITIONS

Session 10

Let's face it, this world is a cold, unfriendly place for a lot of people. If God has moved you into a new area or new situation, let Him use you to bring warmth and light and laughter into your corner of that world. People will love you for it, and you'll love it, too.

You never counted on the road being as rough as it turned out to be? It happens. But maybe you also never counted on a Friend who loves you as much as Jesus. For He Himself has said, "I will never leave you, nor forsake you."

—Smalley and Trent

YOU'RE AIMING TO . . .
- Help families prepare to stay solid under the pressures of change.

YOU'LL STUDY . . .
- Job 1:13-22; 2:7-10; Acts 1:11
- Major themes from Chapter 12 of the book *Home Remedies*

YOU'LL NEED . . .
- Bibles
- Pencils
- Resource 10A, "Traumatic Transitions and Other Family Trials"
- Resource 10B, "Planning Ahead"
- Chalkboard and chalk or newsprint and marker

Step 1 *(5-10 minutes)*

Slow Down for the Speed Bumps
Anticipating Major Family Changes

Write on the board or newsprint: **LIFE = CHANGE**
Ask the group members to agree or disagree.
Hand out "Traumatic Transitions and Other Family Trials" (Resource 10A). After people are done writing, ask two volunteers to tell about a major family change: one who was surprised and unprepared for the change and one who anticipated the change.

What are some typical responses that people have to change? (Surprise, fear, anger, disorientation, loss of perspective, retreat, hiding.) List the answers on the board or newsprint. You will refer to these responses at the end of the session.

Step 2 *(10-15 minutes)*

God Is Not Surprised
Learning by Example

Let's look at one of the most famous Bible characters who experienced rapid-fire, unexpected change.
Have the group read Job 1:13-22; 2:7-10 out loud.

What family changes does Job experience? (He loses all his farm animals—oxen, donkeys, sheep, camels; all his employees are killed; all his children are killed when a windstorm blows down his oldest son's house; his health falls apart.)

Was Job prepared for these transitions? (He may not have been fully prepared emotionally, physically, or financially, although he was a man of great wealth. Yet he was definitely prepared spiritually since, even in bad circumstances, he could worship and praise God.)

What is Job's response to these changing circumstances? (He mourned his loss, worshiped and submitted to God, and did not sin.)

How do Job's wife and friends share in his troubles? (His wife urges him to curse God and die. His friends joined in his grief. They tore their clothes and put dust on their heads. They sat with him in silence for seven days and seven nights.)

We may never endure the changes that Job experienced, but we can be prepared for the transitions our family will inevitably go through, as Smalley and Trent point out.

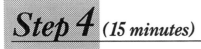

Step 3 (15-17 minutes)

Contingency Plans
Planning Ahead for Change and Disruption

Hand out "Planning Ahead" (Resource 10B) and ask two or three people to read it out loud.

There are many changes that we, as parents, will go through. For example, every new parent has to adjust to less sleep and less time together as a couple. What are some other inevitable changes that parents can anticipate as part of normal family life? (Children starting school, disappointments, success at sports, music, etc., peer pressure, adolescence, physical and emotional changes, dating, empty nest, marriage of children.)

According to this excerpt, how can some of the stress be removed? (Simply by anticipating and planning a course of action for change.)

Allow 3-5 minutes for group members to answer the questions at the bottom of Resource 10B. **What are some of the ways you listed that you can prepare for the changes you anticipate?** (Talk to others who have gone through this phase; read books; pray; search the Scriptures for insights; set aside time to discuss with spouse and make a game plan.)

Change that is anticipated is easier to handle than unexpected change. Yet, as Smalley and Trent point out, we do need to plan for the expected and the unexpected changes. When the unexpected happens, what should we do?

Step 4 (15 minutes)

Facing Transitions
Letting Go—Starting Fresh—Reaching Out

Smalley and Trent suggest "three abiding principles" to cope with transitions. Write these principles on the board or newsprint:

LET GO

START FRESH

REACH OUT

In times of transition or change, what do you think it means to "let go?" (To release the past, our expectations, our plans.)

Imagine that your youngest child is heading off for kindergarten or college (depending on the ages of your group) next week. How will you handle this major transition? (Get a job/more involved in career; do volunteer work; do all the things you've never had time for; travel; begin a women's Bible study; write a book.)

What are some of the things you'll need to release? (A stage of parenting has come to an end; amount of time with the child; amount of influence that you have had on the child; amount of dependency your child has had.)

Smalley and Trent suggest making "this goodbye a significant one. And make it positive!" How can you do this? (Have a party; make a scrapbook of memories and photos; make a video.)

What is the significance of "starting fresh"? (Puts emphasis on the future, suggests hope and new beginnings.)

What's involved in starting fresh? (Replacing old priorities with new priorities; redirecting your energy in new directions; adjusting to a new set of circumstances.)

What are some ways parents of a college-bound child can redirect the energy they've invested in their child? (Get involved in new activities at church, at work, at your health club, or in the community; force yourself to accept a new period of life; don't live in the past, etc.)

The disciples experienced the necessity of starting fresh at the time of Christ's ascension. Have someone read Acts 1:11.

Smalley and Trent paraphrase this verse like this:

"Come on, guys! Why are you standing around gawking into the clouds? Jesus has gone into heaven. That era's over. But get ready! A new era's on the way, and you're a part of it!"

Point to "REACH OUT" on the board and ask, **What do you think it means to reach out?** (Allow God to use you in new ways; get involved with others; use the comfort God has given you to comfort others.)

Referring to the list of reactions to change that the group made in Step 1, ask: **What words might our Lord want to put on this list?** (Let go or yield, begin anew or trust Me with the future, reach out to others.)

Have everyone look back at their answers on Resource 10A. **What was your reaction to the changes you've gone through in the past year? As you look at the changes you can anticipate over the next year, what do you want your response to be?**

Read this quote from the original book: **"Are you faced with a time of transition? Now is the time to reach out to others. Now is the time to make yourself available rather than retreating. Now is the time to seek rather than hide. . . . For (Jesus) Himself has said, 'I will never leave you, nor forsake you.' "**

Close in prayer, asking God to enable each person to trust Him, especially when unexpected change occurs.

TRAGIC TRANSITIONS AND OTHER FAMILY TRIALS

1. Check all the changes your family has experienced in the last year.

- ❑ Bought a new house
- ❑ Renovated an old house
- ❑ Loss of a job
- ❑ New job
- ❑ Major illness (self)
- ❑ Major illness (family member)
- ❑ Death of a spouse
- ❑ Death of extended family member
- ❑ Divorce
- ❑ New baby (birth or adoption)
- ❑ Loss of a child
- ❑ Easing a teenager into adulthood
- ❑ First child entered school
- ❑ Last child left the nest
- ❑ Change of income by $10,000 (+ or -)
- ❑ Change to more active lifestyle
- ❑ Change to less active lifestyle
- ❑ Change in sleeping habits
- ❑ Change in number of disagreements with spouse
- ❑ Other _____
- ❑ Other _____
- ❑ Other _____

2. Of the changes you checked, which was the most significant? Do you feel you were prepared for that change in your life? Why or why not?

PLAN AHEAD

SLOW DOWN

If you haven't figured it out by now, two things are required in preparing for transitions: alert parents and lots of family communication. . . . It's like driving on a road where you see a big orange sign that reads:

CONSTRUCTION AHEAD, NEXT 10 MILES
WATCH FOR FLAGGER
DRIVE WITH EXTREME CAUTION

The wise driver sits up a little straighter, opens his eyes a little wider, and backs off on the accelerator. He knows that at any moment he might have to brake, switch lanes, swerve around a barricade, or slow down for a rough stretch of road.

ANTICIPATE

That's a good way for parents to think about the months and years ahead . . . expect the unexpected . . . anticipate sudden changes in the smooth, straight freeway. *And none of these things should take them by surprise.*

At the Smalley household, Norma and I (Gary) tried to look down the road as much as several years as we attempted to help and encourage our three children. We recognized, for example, that there would be some particularly difficult transitions during the junior years . . . . We wanted to be ready for those speed bumps and treacherous curves in the changes occurring between the ages of eighteen and twenty-two.

In the area of sports, for example, I encouraged my sons by pointing out a family pattern. . . . For some reason, the Smalley male takes a major step in physical maturity at age nineteen. I knew that Greg and Michael would not be motivated in lifting weights or getting stronger and faster until they reached that milestone. . . .

PREPARE

Again and again as my kids have approached various transitions, I've tried to prepare them for what was coming, praise and encourage them through the times of struggle, and give them hope. . . . "It's okay," I tell them, "you're going to get through this and things are going to be so much better you won't believe it. Just wait and see!"

Life IS change. The sooner we accept and *plan on that fact* the more fulfillment and peace we will enjoy in our families. . . . As counselors, we've seen families crumple like wet cardboard simply because they did not anticipate a major transition. Instead of gearing down for a hefty speed bump in the road ahead, some family wagons hit them at ninety miles an hour and rip the axles right off the frame. It doesn't have to be that way.

1. What changes are you anticipating in the lives of your children in the next six months? the next year? (Be specific for each child.)

Child	Next 6 months	Next year
_____	_____	_____
_____	_____	_____
_____	_____	_____
_____	_____	_____

2. How can you prepare for these changes?

WATCHING FOR THE SUNLIGHT

Session 11

I (Gary) grew up in a small town in western Washington state. Every fall and winter I would walk to and from school under a heavy, ever-present blanket of gray. Sometimes the grayness seemed to seep into everything—trees, bushes, buildings, cars, cats, school teachers. There were days in December or January when I began to wonder if anything existed on the other side of those clouds. . . .

Sooner or later, however, the stormy Pacific weather systems rolling off the ocean would pause to catch their breath and I would look up and be startled by a tiny patch of brilliant blue. . . .

Those momentary sun-showers would always lift my spirits. . . .

I experience it still, when I see God's faithfulness break through the gloom of difficult and hurtful life experiences. Whenever I find myself in the darkness of disappointment or puzzling circumstances, I start looking for the sun rays of God's presence and purpose. God has always been faithful in providing that light. . . .

—Smalley and Trent

YOU'RE AIMING TO . . .
- Help families discover positive gain in troubled times.

YOU'LL STUDY . . .
- Psalm 13; Romans 8:28, 35, 38, 39; II Corinthians 4:16-18, 11:23-29, 12:7-10; Hebrews 12:7-11; James 1:2-4
- Major themes from Chapter 13 of the book *Home Remedies*

YOU'LL NEED . . .
- Bibles
- Pencils
- Resource 11A, "Sunlight through the Clouds"
- Resource 11B, "Finding Real Character"
- Chalkboard and chalk or newsprint and marker

Step 1 (5-7 minutes)

The Storm
Anticipating the Clouds

Introduce this session by thinking back to a scene from your own childhood and sharing a stormy experience that God has used to build character in you. Some common scenes: being let down by a friend; failing to make a team or class officer; getting dumped by a girlfriend or boyfriend; struggling with self-image. Keep it short.

Childhood is filled with stormy disappointments. The way we handled these disappointments may still be affecting us! According to Smalley and Trent, "Every family will experience its share of 'cloudy day' hardship and pain. The Bible assures us of that. . . . It's not a matter of IF, it's a matter of WHEN. . . . There is sunlight on the other side of darkness, and those who learn to wait and watch for it will not be disappointed."

Step 2 (10-15 minutes)

Weathering the Storm
Looking for the Sun

Ask the group members to reflect back on their childhood disappointments. **Which stormy scene or trying circumstance comes to mind for you, as if it happened just yesterday?** Be prepared to comment and encourage as needed. You want to avoid lengthy stories. Hand out "Sunlight through the Clouds" (Resource 11A).

Divide the group in two, with one half reading "Terrific Tim" and the other half reading "Finding the Good in the Bad." Have each group answer the questions in light of their respective stories. After 5-7 minutes reconvene as one group and discuss responses to the questions.

(1. Tim's cocky attitude was refined; he matured and became more Christ-like; his life goals changed; he developed a desire to help others. The woman's troubled childhood helped her develop sensitivity and compassion; she's now able to help other troubled children.

2. We should not seek hurt or hardship, and neither should we run from it. Rather we need to be open to God's ability to use it for good in our lives and the lives of our children.

3. Show them by example how good can come from bad. Feel free to share how bad circumstances from childhood resulted in good. If God used your bad circumstances to mature you, be sure to tell that part of the story. Encourage your group members to let God use their hard times and bad circumstances for the benefit of others. Acknowledge that some hurts are very deep and need time, and in some cases, professional help to heal.)

We need to see through our children's trials to see what they can produce in our lives and in the lives of our children.

A Change of Weather
Helping Your Kids See through Their Trials

Hand out "Finding Real Character" (Resource 11B). Have each person fill it out individually. Ask for answers and discussion.

(Some possible answers: [2] Trials, troubles of many kinds, God's correction; [3] It enables us to go through the entire experience without bailing out, makes us mature and complete; [4] As discipline for our good, part of the cost of holiness, part of God's school on righteousness and peace; [5] They reveal our need for God, they teach us about God's faithfulness and sufficiency; [6] Let your children work out their own solutions as much as possible when problems arise; encourage family discussions about what's gone wrong that day; explain that *every trial has value*; pray together about each child's struggles; ask God for wisdom; don't bail your child out of tough situations—let them depend on God for the solution; etc.)

Quote Smalley and Trent: **"The very things we fear might happen to our children can equip them with resilient strength, depending on their response to the challenges."**

The Silver Lining
Letting the Light of Scripture Shine Through

Every cloud has a silver lining. Is this idea scriptural? (Answers may vary, but in essence, yes.) **The apostle Paul and King David knew what it means to experience the Son shining through the storm clouds of life. A mind-set of "this too shall pass or at least get better" is found in the apostle Paul.** Have someone read aloud Romans 8:28, 35, 38, 39. Discuss the importance of the phrase, "who love him, who have been called according to his purpose." This verse may be applied to anyone who has put their faith in Christ for forgiveness. Christians will never be separated from God's love, even if they have major difficulties or trials.

King David gives us another example of sunlight after clouds. Have someone read Psalm 13. Have someone else paraphrase or summarize these six short verses. Point out that David went from the clouds to the sunlight. The key to his quick turnabout is this: *"But I trust in your unfailing love"* (Ps.13:6, NIV). **What better way to see through the clouds than to trust in God's unfailing love! But what about our kids?**

Step 5 (15 minutes)

Sunlight
Enjoying the Sunlight after the Storm

As an answer to the question just raised in Step 3, say: **Here are three ways to help your kids see through the clouds to the sunlight beyond.** Write the three main points (in CAPS) on the board (or on newsprint). Then read the statements that follow.

1. STAY CALM, SPEAK SOFTLY. Think carefully about your very first response to your child's difficult situation. Try calmness and soft-spoken words. How you respond to a situation can determine how traumatic your kids think the situation really is.

Roleplay both parts in this little drama:

<u>Scenario:</u> **One-year-old Johnny has just done a swan dive off the couch.**

<u>Parent Reaction:</u> **Shout "OH NO!" and race across the room.**

<u>Child's Thoughts:</u> **I guess that was pretty bad. I must be hurt. I think I'll scream. I like all this attention. I'll do it again sometime.**

What are some of the traumas your kids deal with? (Accidents, disappointments, romantic heartbreaks, or problems in school.)

What is the effect of calmness and soft-spoken words in the midst of a crisis? (They help your kids think, "Maybe this isn't such a disaster after all.")

Smalley and Trent say: "Knowing ahead of time that God can use hard times to build character into our children's lives can help us keep a grip on our emotions."

2. WATCH FOR DEPRESSION. Keep a watchful eye on your child's responses during and following the traumatizing event.

What are some typical responses that kids have to trauma? (Tears, fear, panic, anger, shock, disappointment, followed by calming down, then acceptance.)

If a child begins to have recurring nightmares, wet the bed, have difficulty concentrating, or have problems at school, he or she needs a parent's help.

As parents, how can we help a child whose reaction goes beyond the norm and heads to depression? (Careful observation. Talk about their feelings. Pray with them. Remind them of God's goodness and constant care. If depression continues, counseling may be necessary.)

3. GET GOD'S VIEWPOINT. A few days after a trial, look for an opportunity to discuss how God could use it in your child's life. Carefully choose the right time to sincerely talk about God's purpose, plan, and love.

What are some good questions to ask to open such a conversation? (Are you satisfied with how you're handling this trial or situation? Can you see anything God may be showing you through this trial? How is it going? Would you like to spend some time thinking through this thing together?)

Point out that you may need to be persistent and remain available until your child is ready to talk.

Where in your Bible might you find comforting words about hard times?

Have your group members develop the last part of this scenario for themselves. If they have trouble with specific references you can direct them to II Corinthians 4:16-18; Hebrews 12:2, 3; Genesis 50:20 or throughout Psalms and Proverbs.

We saw where King David wrote psalms while he was depressed (Psalms

13, 42, 43, etc.), and how he was able to see the silver lining of hope amidst his despair. Paul also went through some very trying times. Have one or two people read II Corinthians 11:23-29.

Now let's see how Paul handled all these problems. Have another person read II Corinthians 12:7-10. What can we learn from Paul's response to trials—even those that are ongoing? (Paul got out of the clouds of despair and took advantage of God's sunlight—God's strength. In Christ, we are strong in our weakness. That's when God can use us best!)

Paul's example challenges us to teach our children to turn their trials and weaknesses into strengths through the power of God. From this week forward, let's help them get out of the clouds and see the sunlight offered us in our life with Christ!

Close in prayer. Thank God that He is always there—especially when things look the darkest.

SUNLIGHT THROUGH THE CLOUDS

Tim Terrific

What can I say about "Tim Terrific"? He was one of those guys who seemed to move in his own private pool of sunlight. He was popular, athletic, and voted "most likely to conquer the solar system." He sailed through college, married a stunning beauty queen, and went to work in a Christian organization—soon soaring to a top post of leadership. Then, following the arrival of two (perfect) daughters, a massive cloud suddenly left their home in shadow. Their third child, a boy, was born with spina bifida.

That was four years ago. Now my friend tells me that the birth of that little boy was the best thing that ever happened to him. I don't know how he and his wife worked through those long gray days of disappointment and strain, but after meeting Tim several weeks ago, I can tell you what he looks like in sunshine.

I could hardly believe I was with the same person. The old cockiness was gone. . . . He seemed more thoughtful, more interested in others, and more loving than I could have believed. Walking with his little boy along a steep, thorny pathway had filled Tim's heart with an unquenchable desire to help others. He left his high-level job to enroll in seminary, heading toward a degree in counseling. All he wants to do with the rest of his life is come alongside people in pain.

Finding the Good in the Bad

She had been sexually molested by both a neighbor and family member as a child. . . . Although a Christian, she struggled constantly with guilt, anger, and low self esteem. For her, every day of life was like waking up to perpetual dusk. . . .

What value could there possibly be in those terrible experiences of her childhood? How could God possibly bring any "sunlight" out of such tragic and evil circumstances? . . . I could see such value in her life—and I firmly believed that God could use even those horrible past events in her life in a positive way.

The truth is, every time you go through a trial like the ones she went through, it gives you qualities of love you would otherwise never have. I spent hours explaining to her how valuable she was. . . .

"You can spot a hurting person a mile away! . . . You're constantly doing things for people. Just looking at you I can see the compassion in your eyes. That's why people come to you with their hurts. . . . They sense right away that you can understand and really *feel* their pain. In fact, your life reads like Hebrews 12:9-11. Because of the hardships you've faced, God has produced a harvest of righteousness (best expressed in love) inside your life."

Finally, she began to see how God could use her—was already using her—in spite of and even *because of* her terrible childhood. She began to smile as the tiniest crevice of blue opened in her cloud cover. It was enough. The sun doesn't need much of an opening.

1. What good came out of the bad circumstances in these stories?

2. How should we respond to hurt or hardship, pain or problems? (See Hebrews 12:9-11.)

3. How then can we guide and nurture our children through the tough times so that they become strong, mature Christians?

Finding Real Character

1. Suppose you had a "Character Qualities Wish List" from which you could draw three qualities for your children to discover and develop over the next year. What three character qualities would you choose to come true for them?

a.

b.

c.

2. Read James 1:2-5. What can actually bring joy to our lives (James 1:2)?

3. What's so important about perseverance (James 1:3-4)?

4. Read Hebrews 12:7-11. How should we view our hardships?

5. How can our problems actually make us stronger Christians? (Give examples from your own life.)

6. List some ideas on helping your children grow through their trials.

CHALLENGE FOR THE WEEK: Help your children see the *benefits* of the trials and troubles that come in their lives.

A FAMILY CONSTITUTION

Vision involves planning for success. It asks questions like, "Where do *we* want to go as a family? What kind of family are *we* going to be? What would *we* like to accomplish in the days and years God gives us together?" If families don't have a standard by which to measure their lives, if they don't have clearly established elements of a successful, happy, mutually satisfying family life, they tend to flounder, *hoping* things work out—rather than *knowing* what it takes to make a healthy home environment.

Drifting without oars may be a pleasant activity for an August afternoon in the middle of a mountain lake. But life isn't a lake; it's a river that's rushing to an end. Smooth, placid stretches of that river will inevitably be shattered by tumbling whitewater rapids or crashing waterfalls.

And a drifting boat manned by a sleeping parent doesn't stand a chance.

—Smalley and Trent

YOU'RE AIMING TO . . .
- Help families develop a family constitution and a vision for their future.

YOU'LL STUDY . . .
- Joshua 22:5; 24:14, 15; Proverbs 29:18; Matthew 20:26-28; Luke 10:27; I Corinthians 12:1, 4, 5
- Major themes from Chapter 12 of the book *Home Remedies*

YOU'LL NEED . . .
- Bibles
- Pencils
- Resource 12A, "Constitutionally Yours"
- Resource 12B, "Our Family Constitution"
- Resource 12C, "Biblical Models or Mandates for Mission"
- Chalkboard and chalk or newsprint and marker

Step 1 *(10-12 minutes)*

Today's Family
Drifting Apart or Holding Together?

I'd like you to close your eyes for a moment and picture this scene. Each member of your family is in a separate little boat on a large lake. There are no oars in the boats and each member is leisurely drifting about wherever the boat takes him or her. After a few hours, you're shocked by the wide distance that Mom and Dad have drifted apart. You're at the opposite end of the lake from where your spouse is. The kids are scattered here and there. A little bit of drifting has created a great separation.

Have the group open their eyes and ask: **If we were to draw a lake and place the "typical Christian family" on it, would their boats be clustered closely together, or would they be scattered?** Allow for varying points of view.

What happened to our family in the first scenario? Why are they all over the lake? (There was no organization or means of staying together. No one was paying attention. They had no plan. There was no way to control their direction.)

If you were to place your own boats in the lake, where would they be? Allow a few brave volunteers to answer. Be honest and share what your family would look like.

Step 2 *(10-15 minutes)*

We the Family
Developing a Foundational Family Constitution

The founding fathers of our country wanted the new nation to be united. To assure this they drafted a document that is still in place as the backdrop of all our government. What is this document called? (The Constitution.)

Has any one ever heard of or thought of writing a Family Constitution? Families who have done so have found it very helpful. Let's take a look at one.

Hand out "Constitutionally Yours," Resource 12A. Point out the two bedrock principles (love and honor God; love and respect others) out of which six simple family limits eventually grew. Have someone read the Smalley Constitution. Then have someone read Luke 10:27.

What does this verse mean? (We are to love God totally, with no reservations or holding back.)

What do you think the value of such a Family Constitution might be? (Sets the course, defines limits, eliminates arguments, gives guidelines, encourages accountability, gives order, offers security.)

How can you keep the Family Constitution central in your home? (Frame it and hang it above the kitchen table, post it on the refrigerator, write the constitution in picture form for young children, talk about it, ask each other questions to keep each other accountable.)

114

Read Proverbs 29:18 from the King James: "Where there is no vision, the people perish." Have someone restate the meaning in their own words.

Hand out Resource 12B and allow couples to work together on their own constitution for about five minutes. Encourage any single parents to work together to brainstorm ideas or group a single parent with a couple. Point out that this activity is just to get them started. Encourage them to finish this activity at home, making it a family project with their children. Make sure that each family has a clean copy to take with them.

Parents will need to explain about a need for unity before the kids are going to buy into this. Make it a positive, exciting adventure of "rowing your boats in the same direction"—not an ugly set of rules.

You'll be amazed how children will thrive with a contract. They'll not only know their limits, but they will have helped create those limits!

Step 3 *(10-15 minutes)*

Serving Together
Seeking God's "Wonderful Plan for Your Life"

After establishing your Family Constitution, you need to settle on your family mission. What does God want your family to do? In a few minutes we will brainstorm some specific ideas. For now, let's look at some Bible passages for some general guidelines.

Hand out "Biblical Models or Mandates for Mission" (Resource 12C). Have someone read the opening quote from Smalley and Trent. Working in small groups, have each group answer the two questions. After 5-10 minutes, discuss the answers within the total group.

Question 1:

Joshua 22:5; 24:14, 15: Love God; walk in His ways; obey His commands; hold fast to God; serve God. Fear God; serve God with all faithfulness; throw away other gods; choose today whom you will serve.

Matthew 20:26-28: Become a servant—if you want to be great in God's eyes.

I Corinthians 12:1, 4, 5: Don't be ignorant of spiritual gifts.

Question 2:

Joshua 22:5; 24:14, 15: Serving God must be part of our mission. God allows us choice. We can serve Him as a team.

Matthew 20:26-28: Serving makes a person great in God's eyes; Jesus came to serve.

I Corinthians 12:1, 4, 5: We should try to determine what gifts God has given us as a family and match our mission to our gift.

What is the one theme that runs throughout all of these verses? (Service of God and other people.)

Point out that God's Word is very encouraging and insightful when it comes to serving together in mission. **When God is the Master of your family, service in His name ceases to be a chore and becomes an exciting adventure. Service can be the key element in keeping your Family Constitution relevant. Service** can also be what keeps your family mission exciting—and what keeps your family together!

Step 4 *(10 minutes)*

Family Mission
What Will We Accomplish as a Family?

God has a plan for each of our families. Point out that Gary Smalley's family finally came to the conclusion that *the family* was the most important element in society—so they dedicated themselves to the job of enriching other families.

What does *your* family feel is important? In what way would your family like to serve God and serve others? What might YOUR family mission be?

Let's make a list of some possible family missions—some things a family could do together as a service or ministry. Point out that a mission is general. Methods are specific ways of fulfilling a mission. Ask for ideas from the group, then write them on the board. Some ideas for starters might be: Equip our children to be effective witnesses in the marketplace; help other people with their physical needs; help the homeless; help improve cross-cultural or cross-racial relations. Find out if any of the families represented already have determined their family mission.

Then take one *mission* idea generated from this springboard discussion and ask the group for specific *methods* to help accomplish that goal. For example, if it is meeting people's physical needs, then we might accomplish that goal by providing food, clothing, medical help, and more. If the family mission is to reach people in other countries with the Gospel, you may suggest they could become missionaries, raise money for other missionaries, pray for foreign missionaries, go on a short-term mission project, etc.

The most important thing is to find the service that everyone in the family can get excited about. With a family mission you become a *team*, working together toward your goal. Gary Smalley says of his family: "We are an army unit, a Green Beret team fighting the enemy that destroys the family."

Step 5 *(10-15 minutes)*

The Five Ms
Giving Our Kids Confidence and Direction

Smalley and Trent suggest that families answer five questions which will help them keep on track. We've talked about mission, which is one of them. Write these words and questions on the board or newsprint:

Master:	Who will we serve?
Mission:	What does God want us to do?
Method:	How will we fulfill our mission?

Maintenance: How will we evaluate and adjust our methods?
Mate: Do Mom and Dad agree about our mission?

How each family answers and communicates about these questions will depend on the age of the children. Brainstorm some ideas for communicating with children of different ages.

For younger children: Use five M&M candies to explain each M. As you finish each M, the child gets to eat the M&M. Make a poster (for the refrigerator, of course) with the five M's. Put large letter M's strategically around the house and let the children guess one of the M's every time they find one of the letters. Then ask your children how they're doing on that M.

For elementary children: Start by telling them that Mom and Dad are trying to live by five M's. Share with them what they are and ask them to be the "police officers" to make sure Mom and Dad stay on track. As they have fun keeping an eye on Mom and Dad's five M's for a while, encourage them to join you in the five M's.

For teens and young adults: Use the five M's as a decision-making aid. Help your teens or young adults arrive at their own conclusions by asking probing questions and listening.

Knowing who you serve and where you're going gives focus to a family. It keeps everyone walking together in the same direction. As your children leave home and start families of their own, it will give them a place to start.

Close with the prayer at the bottom of Resource 12C. Caution your group that the answer will not come overnight. It will take personal prayer, family prayer, and even counsel from others they respect.

CONSTITUTIONALLY YOURS

Smalley Family Constitution

We the people of the Smalley family,
in order to form a more perfect union,
do establish these *two basic principles:*

1. Love and honor God.
2. Love and respect others.

We hereby base these principles on the
Word of God (Luke 10:27).

We also hereby establish *six family
limits* from these two principles:

1. We honor Mom and Dad by obeying them.
2. We honor others and our possessions by putting
things away after we have used them.
3. We honor our commitment to the family by
performing all chores responsibly.
4. We honor friends and family by having good
manners and exercising responsibility toward others.
5. We honor all of God's creation;
people and things.
6. God is worthy to receive our highest honor
and praise, and His Word is to be honored as well.

Dated: _____

Signed: _____   _____
        Mom   Dad   _____

_____   _____   _____
  Michael   Kari   Greg

OUR FAMILY CONSTITUTION

Our Family Constitution

We the people of the _____ family, in order to form a more perfect union, do establish these two basic principles:

1. Love and honor God.
2. Love and respect others.

We hereby base these principles on the Word of God (Luke 10:27).

We also hereby establish six family limits from these two principles:

1.

2.

3.

4.

5.

6.

Dated: _____

Signed:

BIBLICAL MODELS OR MANDATES FOR MISSIONS

Resource 12C

"If you don't have a clearly-defined direction as a family, other people or the crush of life's circumstances will tend to set it for you. You will find yourself the slave of other people and circumstances rather than following your own clearly established, defined decisions."

—*Smalley and Trent*

Read the following passages: Joshua 22:5; 24:14, 15; Matthew 20:26-28; I Corinthians 12:1, 4, 5. Then answer these questions.

1. What biblical models or mandates do you see here?

2. What do these models or mandates say about family mission?

A Family Prayer

"What is it, Lord, that You would like us to accomplish as a family? We know that our time together on this earth is limited. We know that You have a plan for us. We know that Your Word says the two most important things in all of life are to love and honor God, and to love and honor people. We want to honor people by serving them, but what do You want us to do *specifically*?"

THE UNFAILING WELL

Session 13

At some point in each of our life's journeys, we grind our fenders into something like a cement retaining wall. It's the hard, unyielding fact that "life is not fulfilling." To the contrary, it is often unjust, unpalatable, and rarely lives up to its billing. We can *never* siphon enough emotional energy or sense of significance from others, locations, or things to keep our personal buckets overflowing. Even though billboards promise "You'll be satisfied," we never are.

In fact, by so diligently pursuing people, places, and things, we end up with the very feelings of anxiety, fear, uncertainty, and confusion we've been trying to avoid. Nothing falls as hard or shatters into as many pieces as a high expectation that runs headlong into cold reality.

—Smalley and Trent

YOU'RE AIMING TO . . .
■ Help parents handle their disappointments in a way that will powerfully impact the peace and stability of their home.

YOU'LL STUDY . . .
■ Isaiah 55:1-3, 12; Jeremiah 2:13; John 4:13, 14; 7:37-39; 10:10
■ Major themes from Chapter 13 of the book *Home Remedies*

YOU'LL NEED . . .
■ Bibles
■ Pencils
■ Resource 13A, "Review of Symptoms and Remedy"
■ Resource 13B, "Down at the Well"
■ Resource 13C, "How Am I Doing?"
■ Chalkboard and chalk or newsprint and marker
■ Candy or gum as prizes (optional)

Step 1 *(5-15 minutes)*

Review
Matching a Remedy to the Symptoms

This first step reviews the previous twelve home remedies and anticipates Remedy No. 13. For your own preparation as a leader, check through your notebook and this leader's guide, so that you can "fill in the blanks" for people who missed one or more sessions. Depending on available time, you have several options for using "Review of Symptoms and Remedy" (Resource 13A).

FIRST OPTION (15 minutes): Divide into two groups. Have each group list as many of the twelve principles or remedies as they can in three minutes. After "checking the lists" give a small prize (piece of candy or gum, etc.) to each member of the winning team. Delay handing out "Review of Symptoms and Remedy" Resource 13A, until after this activity.

SECOND OPTION (10 minutes): Hand out "Review Quiz on Symptoms and Remedy" (Resource 13A) and use as follows: Fold the right-hand edge over to the left to cover up just the **Remedy** column, without covering the **Symptoms** column. Have group members write their own remedies on the flap before peeking underneath to discover the authors' cure.

THIRD OPTION (5 minutes): Simply hand out Resource 13A, so your group does not have to take notes, nor a quiz, nor tax their memory. They can just read it and file it away as a book review.

Step 2 *(10-15 minutes)*

Three Wells
Looking for the Good Things in Life

After twelve sessions discovering the remedies to all your home ailments, I suppose all the families represented here have it made! Right?. . . Wouldn't it be nice if it were that simple? Just when we think we've got it all together, Satan slips his foot in the door and messes things up.

Recall recent trials and tribulations from the life of group members you know. Otherwise, suggest typical examples: the bike gets stolen, the new puppy puddles on the carpet, the boyfriend or girlfriend suddenly forgets his or her undying love, our family expectations are dashed. End by underscoring this one: **The result? Our well runs dry.**

Most people dip into one of three wells to find their satisfaction, especially when disappointments come to your family. Hand out "Down at the Well" (Resource 13B). Read the excerpt from the book out loud as a group. Then have them fill in the things they draw out of these three wells. (Suggested items: OTHERS include spouse, kids, new friend, work associates, an emotional affair. LOCATIONS include beautiful home, exciting vacation, living in a certain place, good circumstances. THINGS include money, new house or car, better job, computer games.)

Point out, as Smalley and Trent do, that it is easy to rely on things we can see and touch to fill our emotional buckets. It's also easy to depend on spouse or children to meet all of our relational needs. **It's not wrong to enjoy other people, fun locations, or material things. The problem comes when we depend on them looking for lasting happiness. Why doesn't this work?** (God programmed us to need Him. We cannot be satisfied apart from Him. A bigger house only provides temporary happiness. Pinning all our happiness on another person can only lead to future disappointment.)

When disappointment or depression comes, and it will, the heavenly remedy must be applied to your home situation. So how do we avoid having our well run dry? Smalley and Trent offer three tips:

1. Identify your felt needs. Looking at Resource 13B and the things we listed by the well from which we most often draw may help.

2. Release your wrong expectations. To quote Smalley and Trent: "It might even help to say out loud, 'I value my friend, but I can't expect her to make me happy,' or 'I like watching movies on the VCR, but it doesn't bring me lasting joy.'"

3. Draw upon Christ. He is the one well that does satisfy.

Step 3 *(10-15 minutes)*

The Well of Living Water
Drawing upon Christ and Drinking from Him

Assign a different reader for each of the verses listed. Cover the verses and questions one at a time.

Isaiah 55:1-3,12: **What is God's gracious provision for our lasting benefit?** (A "heaven remedy" that God offers to us free of charge; we cannot earn it nor pay for it. For whatever ails us, the cure is God's grace, and the result is everlasting joy and peace.)

Jeremiah 2:5-8: **In Jeremiah's day, what was wrong with God's people?** (They forgot the God of their fathers, turned to worthless idols, and rebelled against God.)

How are we like the Israelites? (In our search for happiness, we often don't look to the source of happiness—God. Our own wells of things, others, and locations eventually run dry, or our buckets get holes in them.)

John 4:13, 14: **At Jacob's well, who is the "living water"?** (Jesus.)

How long will Jesus' water satisfy? (Forever. To quote Smalley and Trent: "When we dip into Christ and drink from Him, it becomes a well of water within us that continually overflows.")

John 7:37-39: **What is the prerequisite for receiving the streams of living water?** (Cultivate a spiritual thirst, or desire, and believe in Jesus Christ.)

Who is this stream of living water that flows from within every believer? (The Holy Spirit flows from within.)

Why does Jesus refer to the Spirit as living water? (Unlike any other kind of water supply, this one satisfies our spiritual thirst, not just our felt needs. The Spirit is powerful, active, cleansing, eternal.)

John 10:7-10: **What is the only remedy that is full to overflowing?** (God in Christ is the source of abundant life.)

Point out that this stream of living water can flow continually from each of your homes, as long as you draw from Jesus' well. Lasting contentment and satisfaction can only come from living by the power of the Holy Spirit!

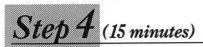 *(15 minutes)*

The Bottom Line
Evaluating Progress in Applying *Home Remedies*

1. Be sure each family member has trusted in Christ as Savior. If someone has not yet done this, first make sure s/he knows that Jesus is the only way, the truth, and the life—that no one comes to God except through Jesus (see John 14:6). Then pray for that person daily.

2. Be sure to draw from Christ's overflowing well of living water to satisfy your own needs, so that you can successfully apply the "Home Remedies" that we have been studying.

Hand out "How Am I Doing?" (Resource 13C). Let group members fill it in silently. Assure them that they will not be sharing their answers. This is a self-evaluation form to evaluate their own family situations and determine what remedies are needed in their family.

Close in prayer, asking God to guide and protect each family represented. Pray that each family will use the remedies we've studied in these thirteen sessions. Pray that they will find their happiness in the *living water* offered by Jesus to all who believe.

REVIEW OF SYMPTOMS AND REMEDIES

NOTE: Certain sessions will be better remembered by activities and stories (remember the Lion, Otter, Golden Retriever, and Beaver?) than by the symptoms or remedy classification used by the authors. Don't worry about getting the wording exactly like the authors. The point is to review which symptoms suggest which remedies.

	Child's Symptoms	**Home Remedy**
1	Low self-esteem, deep discouragement, feeling unloved	Treasuring
2	Heavy heart, unrealized potential, chronic mediocrity; distress, fear, loneliness, feelings of detachment	Affirmation and Meaningful Touch
3	Lack of discipline, dishonesty, self-centeredness	Fairness and Consistency
4	Emotional "drift," frustration, arguments	Meaningful Communication
5	Personality conflicts, ridicule, finger-pointing, relational strain, constant comparisons, misunderstandings	Valuing and Blending Our Differences
6	Distance, darkness, unforgiveness	Untying Anger Knots
7	Escalating conflict, unwilling listener, wrong conclusions	Attack Issues, Not People; Use Word Pictures
8	Nothing in common, lack of closeness, no family memories	Shared Experiences
9	Long-standing problems, no follow-through, lonely struggles	Accountability, Support Groups
10	Transition shock, disorientation, loss of perspective	Let Go, Fresh Start, Reach Out
11	Depression, bewilderment, crushing disappointment	Watching for Sunlight
12	Traveling in circles, disintegrating family, constant confusion	Vision; A Family Constitution
13	Emptiness, dissatisfaction, disillusionment	The Unfailing Well

DOWN AT THE WELL

Resource 13B

It's easy to find examples in every family of how we look to others, locations, and things for fulfillment. Parents often attempt to live vicariously through the successes of their children. Dad may be a frustrated athlete pushing his son to star in Little League. Mom may have dreamed of singing at the Met and so nags her daughter to practice music for hours every day. A parent wanting a child to land a lucrative career demands straight A's in school so that she'll qualify for a scholarship at one of the 'right' schools.

A child may face the same dilemma. He desperately wants the approval of his father, so he's crushed when dad fails to praise his three hits in the game—but instead criticizes him for striking out the fourth time. We counsel scores of adults who are still desperately trying to achieve the approval of their parents. If they could only gain that approval, they reason, their bucket would finally be filled.

Lacking parental acceptance, children may look for happiness in things like computer games, fashionably correct clothing, a group of friends, or a complete stereo system for their room. They learn soon enough that they never have enough 'stuff,' so they beg for more. The pattern may haunt them into adulthood. Other kids may reason a *place* will fill their buckets—any place but home! So they run away, or apply to a college across the country, or take a job and find a run-down apartment with a friend.

. . . If your ultimate goal in a marriage or in a family is to say to your husband or wife or children, 'I need life from you. Will you meet my needs and keep my bucket full?' you are asking for huge problems . . . and profound disappointment.

. . . How you handle these disappointments as a parent will have a powerful impact on the peace and stability of your home.

Most people dip into three wells to find their satisfaction.
1. Which well do you dip into *most* often to satisfy your needs?
2. What needs do you draw upon this well to fulfill?
3. Which well is the *least* satisfying to you and why?
4. What might cause these wells to go dry?

HOW AM I DOING?

Circle T for a True response. Circle F for a False response.

T   F   1. My children and spouse know how valuable they are to me.

T   F   2. I am encouraging my children through word and meaningful touch.

T   F   3. I am trying to teach my children to be honest and serve others.

T   F   4. The atmosphere in my home is becoming more fair and consistent.

T   F   5. I'm creating opportunities for my family to talk together.

T   F   6. Each member of my family is different, but we're working as a team.

T   F   7. I'm continuing to untie my anger knots in my home.

T   F   8. When there's a conflict at home, I'm attacking the ISSUE, not the PERSON or the RELATIONSHIP.

T   F   9. I'm giving family activities top priority on my calendar.

T   F   10. I'm looking to God and other Christians for support and counsel.

T   F   11. I'm starting to plan ahead for those transitions my family will go through.

T   F   12. I'm helping my children see through the clouds of trials to the sunlight found in Christ.

T   F   13. My family has established and signed a Family Constitution.

T   F   14. I know who my Master is.

T   F   15. I know my mission in life.

T   F   16. Each member of my family has trusted in Jesus as Savior.

T   F   17. I'm praying daily for my family.

T   F   18. My family knows what we want to accomplish as a family.

T   F   19. I'm not depending on others, locations, or things for lasting happiness.

T   F   20. I am drinking from God's well, that never runs dry, for personal and family happiness.

Between you and God: Use this list as prayer requests.
Ask God to help you where you marked false.
Trust that He will.

Want to publicize your course on *Home Remedies*? Bring in additional group members by using these reproducible helps. Feel free to copy the bulletin insert below and the sign on the next page. Fill in the dates, time, location, and leader, and customize as you wish.

HOME REMEDIES
Timeless Prescriptions for Today's Family

What kind of home do you want your children to look back on years from now? Will the word "home" stir memories of warmth, laughter, and deep-felt love? Is it the kind of place where your spouse would rather be with you than at work or with others . . . the kind of place where hurting friends and neighbors find God's love and support?

—Gary Smalley and John Trent in *Home Remedies*

Want to find out how to heal hurts and prevent ailments in your family? Whether you are a parent of a newborn or a young adult, come and learn timeless prescriptions for your family with *Home Remedies*.

DATES:

TIME:

LOCATION:

LEADER:

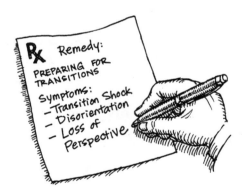

This course is based on the book *Home Remedies* by Gary Smalley and John Trent, published by Multnomah Press.

HOME REMEDIES
Timeless Prescriptions for Today's Family

What kind of home do you want your children to look back on years from now? Will the word "home" stir memories of warmth, laughter, and deep-felt love? Is it the kind of place where your spouse would rather be with you than at work or with others . . . the kind of place where hurting friends and neighbors find God's love and support?

—Gary Smalley and John Trent in *Home Remedies*

Want to find out how to heal hurts and prevent ailments in your family? Whether you are a parent of a newborn or a young adult, come and learn timeless prescriptions for your family with *Home Remedies*.

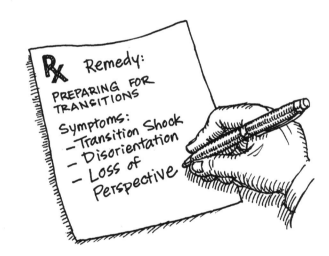

DATES:

TIME:

LOCATION:

LEADER:

This course is based on the book *Home Remedies* by Gary Smalley and John Trent, published by Multnomah Press.